Smallmouth Strategies
for the Fly Rod

Smallmouth Strategies for the Fly Rod

WILL RYAN

Illustrations by Chris Armstrong

LYONS & BURFORD, PUBLISHERS

To my mom and dad,
who have been a constant source of support
for my ventures in print and astream.
Thanks so very much.

Printed in the United States of America

10 9 8 7 6 5 4 3 2 1

Design by MRP Design

Library of Congress Cataloging-in-Publication Data

Ryan, Will, 1951–
    Smallmouth strategies for the fly rod / Will Ryan.
        p.   cm.
    Includes bibliographical references and index.
    ISBN 1-55821-343-0 (cloth)
    1. Smallmouth bass fishing. 2. Fly fishing. I. Title.
SH681.R93   1996
799.1'758—dc20   95-48196
                                   CIP

Contents

Acknowledgments

Authors are often portrayed as snooty and superior, but in fact writing a book is a very humbling undertaking.

Many people have been very helpful to me along the way. I'd like to thank photographer Bill Thuss for his fine work on the color plates; artist Chris Armstrong for his lifelike drawing; and the entire staff at Lyons & Burford for their commitment to this project and invaluable contribution to the final product. David Green of the New York State Department of Environmental Conservation sent me some very interesting research material. Dr. Mark Ridgway, fisheries researcher at Algonquin Provincial Park, spent a good deal of time discussing the ideas in this book with me, and I am grateful for his interest. Both Bob Clouser and Dave Wolff provided good information on the fishing in the Susquehanna Valley. Bill Hyatt, supervisor of fisheries management for the Connecticut Fish and Wildlife Department, and Pete Mirick, information and education specialist, from the Massachusetts Division of Fisheries and Wildlife, have always taken time from busy days to answer my questions. Bob Clouser, Bob Long Jr., Joe Messinger Jr., and Art Scheck were all kind enough to send me flies to use in the color plates.

My friends on the Hampshire College faculty have been quite tolerant of my ramblings about bass fishing. Aaron Berman, David Kerr, Mark Feinstein, and Merle Bruno were helpful at various points. I've benefited immensely from working with other writing teachers at Hampshire, including Debbie Berkman, Nina Payne, Lynne Hanley, Deb Gorlin, and Ellie Siegel. Ray Coppinger and Stan Warner deserve special mention, not only for the interest they share in the relation of humans to wildlife and fisheries, but also for the passion they bring to the pursuit of everything that swims.

Bob Elman, Joe Healy, Bob McNitt, Art Scheck, Ralph Stuart, and Mike Toth provided encouragement and friendship from the editorial side of the writing desk. My editor for this book, Jim Babb, has been more than patient with my deliberate pace and clear in his explanations.

I want to give special thanks to Steven B. Oates, my graduate school advisor, who taught me so much about writing, in particular how to write for an audience beyond academia; and to my old friend Peter Eddy, for his insight, humor, and delight in the well-turned phrase.

People often think of the writer's life as full of socializing and such, but the reality is we're largely solitary drones. I don't have a lot of friends in the writing world, but I do have three good ones: Tom Fuller from Massachusetts, Mark Scott from Vermont, and Tony Zappia from upstate New York. Thanks, guys. Where should we spend all the money?

My great-Aunt Margaret used to worry that fishing would ruin my life; her prescience should not go unrecognized. Along these lines, I know I should thank all my smallmouth bass fishing buddies, though I'm not sure why: Don Bechaz, Pete Bellinger, Steve Boyer, Steve Charles, Mark Craig, Ted Creighton, Lee Ellsworth, Morgan Grant, Shawn Gregoire, Amy Hines, Greg Hooper, Scott Johnson, John Kaufman, Jack Kuzjiac, Jack LaHare, Kurt Lanning, the late Buzz LaRose, Ted Lehnert, Ken Leon, Christian Loftus, Pete Loftus, the late Dave Nolan, Ralph Ringer, Marcel Rocheleau, Scott Smith, and the late Ron "Tate" Tatro.

I'd like to thank my Aunt Elsie and Uncle Bob for letting me keep my ratty old boat at their dock on the river for all these years; and I'd also like to thank my friend Janice Charles for letting me keep all my ratty old fishing friends in her cottage.

Most of all, I need to thank Noreen and Brody. You guys are great; you mean the world to me.

Introduction

W hile many fly fishers go after smallmouth bass, relatively little has been written on the subject, particularly when compared with the heavenly prose offered up to trout and salmon, and lately to saltwater species.

That's starting to change. The last ten years have seen a spate of magazine articles and a book (and parts of several others) devoted to fly fishing for smallmouths; still, the subject seems somehow underrepresented. Perhaps that's because much of the information, however useful, focuses on stream smallmouths, on fishing for bass in places where they behave the most like trout.

Here's where I wade in to cover the bigger waters: rivers, flowages, reservoirs, and lakes. There is information in this book on fishing "trout-stream smallmouths"—hellgrammites, for example, have long fascinated me—but my love is the big waters.

Since the literature largely ignores big-water smallmouth fishing, there's a lot to say, starting with a great deal about the fish itself—its life cycle, behavior, forage, and seasonal and daily movements. This book draws heavily on existing scientific research, for if fishing writers have been silent on these matters, fishing researchers have been anything but. Their findings are fascinating.

I assume readers can tie knots, cast, make presentations, handle line; I assume a basic familiarity with forage types, fly categories, and the principles of fly fishing in general. I spend more time on the "smallmouth" side of smallmouth fly fishing—in other words, leaning more on the insight of other smallmouth anglers—than on the liturgy of fly fishing for trout. Bait and lure fishers have some very useful ideas about how to catch more and bigger smallmouths. And there is no trout canon to extrapolate from when you're drifting over a gravel shoal in 20 feet of water and the angler next to you is knockin' 'em silly with pink Mister Twisters.

*   *   *

It used to be that a good bass-bugging rod could double as a home defense system, but modern materials mean that a 6- to 7- weight rod will handle just about any smallmouth bug or popper you'd want to throw. Actually, though, the more significant tackle innovations involve high-density lines and sinking tips. These lines allow anglers to reach the depths needed to take smallmouths right through the summer.

Along with improvements in tackle has come a larger movement to take fly rods places they've never been. In New England's biggest lakes and New York's Lake George, Finger Lakes, and New York City reservoirs; the entire Great Lakes system and myriad midwestern lakes and rivers; the TVA reservoirs in the South and the major rivers across the land—the Umpqua, Snake, and Columbia in the West and the Hudson, Connecticut, and Delaware in the East—people are fly fishing for smallmouth bass in numbers never seen before.

A driving force behind the smallmouth renaissance has been improved water quality in the lower stretches of trout rivers throughout the country. Smallmouths tolerate warmer water than trout and have thus flourished in sections of rivers that formerly struggled to hold catfish and carp. This has had a particular impact in the East; trout fishing has declined simultaneously with smallmouth fishing's improvement.

The smallmouth's capacity for living in the shadow of industrialism, long touted as an important dimension of its character, has indeed been a source of strength for the species. Today, fly fishers on shore and in small boats find excellent Lake Michigan smallmouth angling inside the city limits of Chicago. In the East, excellent smallmouth fishing exists within commuting distance of every major city. The Delaware, the Mohawk and Hudson, the Connecticut, and the Susquehanna all flow through their respective state capitals—the Potomac flows through our nation's capital; each offers exceptional smallmouth fishing virtually within sight of downtown.

This book owes a great deal to all these developments as well as to the increasing interest in fly fishing for smallmouth bass, the growing awareness that smallmouth angling is superior to fishing for stocked trout—not only in the fight of the fish, but in the complexity of the experience.

As we will see, this is less a new idea than a return to an old one.

*   *   *

I've always thought that books about fishing are as much about people as they are about fish. We like to think of fishing as a natural thing, but it really is a constructed one—exquisitely constructed, but constructed nonetheless. So this book also tells the story of the angling community's relationship with smallmouth bass. My interest cen-

Pound for pound the gamest fish that swims.

ters less on who discovered what fly when and more on how we've come to see the smallmouth as we do. How is it, for instance, that we hold fishing tournaments for smallmouth bass and designate catch-and-release sections of rivers for trout?

To fly fishers, bass are the "other fish," always were, always will be. They are dumb, but fighters—or so goes the anthropomorphization.

There is a certain logic to seeing the smallmouth as an unsophisticated form of trout if you fish the former hoping it'll substitute for the latter. Often, that's how fly fishers drift into smallmouth angling.

Actually, smallmouths are opportunistic feeders. They're less selective than trout because they're different, not because they're less sophisticated. It's a little like complaining that your fly rod doesn't handle Jitterbugs quite as well as your dad's old bait-casting rod, or that your Labrador retriever has a tough time pointing grouse.

If you're reading a book about smallmouth bass you must already have an interest in fishing for them. So the importance of understanding the image of smallmouths may come down to the ways that it has over the years circumscribed fishing strategies.

For that, I refer you to the biology and principles of smallmouth fishing in chapters 3 and 4 in hopes of establishing a foundation that is a modification of neither trout fishing on the one hand nor largemouth fishing on the other. Chapter 5 goes into gear and flies.

The first five chapters constitute an introductory part of the book. In them certain discussions—feeding behavior is a good example—go only so far. I attend to the specifics of various smallmouth forage, behaviors, habitat, and strategies in the remaining chapters.

The second part of the book unfolds seasonally: spring (chapter 6), summer (chapters 7–12), fall (chapter 13). The chapters organize around forage groups and water types.   *   *   *

I grew up in northern New York in the 1950s and '60s, and nobody I knew thought twice about smallmouth bass—except me. Somehow I became a bass fisherman in a fly-fishing culture that venerated salmonids.

Ernest Hemingway maintained that the best training for a writer was an unhappy childhood. If so, I am eminently prepared to write a book on fly fishing for smallmouth bass. (Relax, Mom. I had a wonderful childhood; it's only the smallmouth part that held trauma.)

I write about how people view smallmouth bass. I don't lobby for bass as overlooked gamefish, however, or at least I try to avoid it. And I really don't care if more people start fishing smallmouths, though I do hope for a greater recognition of the complexity involved in their pursuit. Smallmouths have been on the American fly-fishing scene for more than two centuries. That much they have coming.

1 Beginnings...

I n 1785 one Robert Hunter Jr., a visitor to the area around Montreal, described in his diary the excellent angling in the nearby rivers. It was nothing, apparently, for fly fishermen to catch three dozen fish in a half hour. Smallmouth bass, that is.

Although smallmouths were noted in a report on the St. Lawrence valley written in 1664 as well as in a Jesuit's account of the Great Lakes in 1761, Hunter's diary entry is the first mention of fly fishing for them. Fishing historian Paul Schullery calls it the second reliable reference to fly fishing in the New World. It should come as little surprise that the fly-fishing community has not exactly embraced this moment as a cornerstone of its heritage.

If nothing else, the incident underscores the extent to which fishing was and is an intensely localized activity. For our purposes, just because little is written about fly fishing for smallmouths in the Northeast before the late nineteenth century doesn't mean no one was doing it.

The bass were certainly ready and willing. Smallmouths, in fact, are indigenous to North America, having originated in the Great Lakes drainage during the late Pleistocene era some twenty thousand years ago.

For the most part, the Minnesota River watershed represented the northwestern limit of their original distribution. The upper Mississippi River and related tributaries had smallmouths, too. Their southwestern range extended from Minnesota to central Iowa, through north central Missouri, down into the Ozark rivers of eastern Oklahoma, central Missouri, and southwestern Arkansas.

DISTRIBUTION OF BLACK BASSES

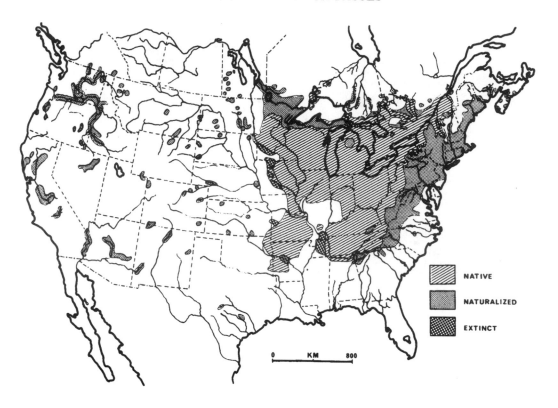

NATIVE

NATURALIZED

EXTINCT

0   KM   800

The smallmouth bass has spread far beyond its original distribution, as indicated by this 1975 map.

Smallmouths swam in streams and rivers throughout Kentucky, Tennessee, Ohio, and western Pennsylvania. The Appalachian Mountains blocked their spread to coastal areas. Their farthest penetration east came in the north, via Lake Ontario and the St. Lawrence River (including tributaries to the north), which afforded them access to Lake Champlain and Lake George.

As such, the smallmouth's native range remained largely out of reach of eighteenth-century anglers, who devoted most of their attention to the brook trout. The earliest smallmouth fly fishing activities in North America (there were no bass in Europe) most likely involved incidents similar to the one described in Mr. Hunter's journal.

In the early nineteenth century the smallmouth in Lake Ontario, the St. Lawrence River, and Lake Champlain, as well as in Kentucky and Tennessee, developed a reputation as a sportfish. There are references to trolling with flies, but for the most part the fishing probably involved live bait.

A few anglers did fish with flies, however, and events of the nineteenth century would conspire to make a tradition of it. The Erie Canal carried smallmouths across central New York in 1825. To the south, smallmouths crossed the Appalachian Mountains just before the Civil War, taking up residence in the waters around the nation's capital. After the war, private citizens, in concert with state agencies, introduced smallmouths into New England.

Then, in 1881, Dr. James Henshall published *Book of the Black Bass,* the first significant book on bass fishing. Henshall wrote of largemouths and smallmouths and, like a parent, strove to show equal affection to both. Nevertheless, he clearly had his favorite—the smallmouth—and it showed.

Henshall explained the various approaches to fishing for bass but took pains to position himself as a fly fisher and fly fishers as gentlemen. He wrote with authority on patterns and strategies for fly fishing. And, with modern rod-and-reel design a hot topic of the day, Henshall promoted his own "Henshall Black Bass Minnow Rod" and devoted considerable discussion to the appropriate black bass fly rod, a 9- to 11-foot wand.

What distinguished Henshall's prose, however, was less the technical subject matter than his enthusiasm for the sporting quality of the black bass. "Inch for inch and pound for pound, the gamest fish that swims" does not exactly stand as an equivocal statement, even given the rhetorical nature of magazine writing in the latter part of the nineteenth century. It may be the most quoted line in American sportfishing. And with it Henshall ensured his place in fishing history as the father of black bass fishing.

Interest in smallmouth fishing surged, and a burgeoning rail system distributed smallmouths clear to the West Coast. California, Kansas, Nevada, and Wyoming stocked

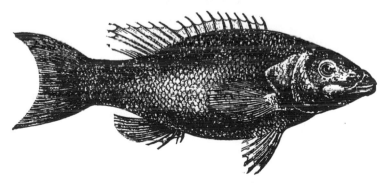

MICROPTERE DOLOMIEU.

The smallmouth bass, as it appeared in Dr. James Henshall's Book of the Black Bass.

The St. Lawrence River remains one of the grand smallmouth waters in this country.

their waters with smallmouths in the 1880s. By the turn of the century, smallmouths swam in lakes and rivers around the country, except for the deep South.

With a pride in technology that would become numbingly banal a century later, sporting gentlemen of the era pointed to the clanking, belching locomotive, the machine that made it all possible. General William Shriver's letter of 1860, which described how the Potomac River was stocked with thirty bass, exemplified this "thanks to modern technology" motif:

> The enterprise or experiment was contemplated by me long before the completion of the Baltimore and Ohio Railroad to the Ohio River at Wheeling, but no satisfactory mode of transportation presented itself to my mind until after the completion of the great work (in, I believe, the year 1853), and

in the following year I made my first trip (although I made several afterwards in the same year), carrying with me my first lot of fish in a large tin bucket, perforated, and which I made to fit the opening in the water-tank attached to the locomotive, which was supplied with fresh water at the regular water stations along the line of the road, and thereby succeeded well in keeping the fish (which were young and small, having been selected for the purpose) alive, fresh, and sound.

Smallmouths were not the only fish carried by rail. Trout and other species traveled in a similar fashion. The point, as always, remains what people made of it. In Shriver's rendition, the locomotive not only transported smallmouths, but nurtured them as well.

"The black bass is peculiarly adapted," Henshall noted, "in every respect, for stocking inland waters. There is no fish that will give more abundant and satisfactory returns, and none in which the labor and expense attending its introduction is so slight."

The brook trout had flourished in virgin America, but, as Henshall observed, it was simply not up to the pressures of modern living: ". . . In this utilitarian age its days are numbered and its fate irrevocably sealed. As the red man disappears before the tread of the white man, the 'living arrow' of the mountain streams goes with him . . . iron has entered its soul. As the buffalo disappears before the iron horse, the brook trout vanishes before the axe of the lumberman. . . ."

The bass had the fortitude to swim, in Henshall's words, "in open public waters . . . to withstand, and defy, many of the causes that will, in the end, effect the annihilation and extinction of the brook trout."

"The black bass," Henshall explained further, "is eminently an American fish, and has been said to be representative in his characteristics. He has the faculty of asserting himself and making himself completely at home wherever placed. He is plucky, game, brave, and unyielding to the last when hooked."

An Horatio Alger hero if ever there were one, the bass was fish perfected: mechanized, hardy, American. Any doubt, then, that the bass was "the fittest to survive the changes and mutations consequent on the march of civilization . . ."?

As things turned out, the smallmouth certainly lived up to Henshall's prediction. The smallmouth's problem was not what it was, but what it wasn't—namely, longed for, desired, romanticized. Even Henshall knew that "the trout is essentially a creature of the pine forests. Its natural home is in waters shaded by pine balsam, spruce, and hemlock, where the cold mountain brooks retain their low temperature, and the air is redolent with balsamic fragrance; where the natural food of the trout is produced in the greatest abundance, and where its breeding grounds are undisturbed."

Wealthy anglers took trips from Boston to Maine or from New York to the Adirondacks to fish for native brook trout, symbols of the receding virgin wilderness, using methods handed down from the English upper class. The experience was at once unsoiled and aristocratic—perfect, in other words.

Smallmouths, by contrast, flourished as a result of technology, swam in the shadow of industrialism, were caught with new fishing methods generated by American know-how. Bass became the fish next door. Good peasant stock of midwestern origins. Hayseeds. Utterly adaptable.

To sporting gentlemen, trout were rare and noble, delicately sipping flies from the surface. Bass were common, boorish gluttons. Trout were streamlined and smooth skinned. Bass, blunt shaped with coarse scales. Without class. These assumptions echoed more pernicious beliefs of the day about racial superiority; this was the era of Jim Crow and immigration from eastern Europe and Asia, and perhaps that lent them

Thanks to Henshall's promotion and the spread of smallmouths into new regions, more and more fly fishers became bass fishermen in the late nineteenth century.

a resonance they would not have enjoyed at other times. Be that as it may, these sentiments left an indelible mark on fly fishing for smallmouth bass.

As it stood, Henshall, Louis Rhead, and other prominent fishing writers continued to trumpet the virtues of fly fishing for smallmouths. In print the debate fell largely along the lines of which fish was superior. Antismallmouth sentiment per se, which would become fairly widespread in the Northeast by the midtwentieth century, may actually have been quite mild in the late nineteenth and early twentieth centuries.

The Maine Fish Commission report (1867) warned of the danger of stocking them in trout water. Otherwise, smallmouths got a nice introduction: "They will increase as rapidly as perch, and as a table fish and affording sport in their capture, rank in the first class."

Even more telling is an excerpt from a 1903 book entitled *The Basses, Freshwater and Marine* (edited by Louis Rhead). The author, William Harris, greeted enthusiastically the smallmouth's presence in the Beaverkill near Roscoe, noting that "at the junction of the east branch of the Delaware River and the Beaverkill, 150 miles from New York City, and all along the first-named water to Hancock, a distance of about 12 miles, some of the best fly-fishing for black bass in New York or any other state can be found."

The trout fishermen he encountered on the Beaverkill simply fished around the bass.

Indeed, as late as the 1930s, in areas so infused with brookie sentiment as the Adirondacks, smallmouth bass seemed less vilified than ignored. In his book on fishing in the Adirondacks during the 1930s, Victor Engels explained that, while some anglers preferred the trout to the bass, he found both fish quite enjoyable. He wrote with enthusiasm of catching 2-pound smallmouths in the Raquette River on small nymphs.

The key to attitudes regarding the smallmouth, I think, was the status of brook

Dr. James Henshall, the father of the black bass.

trout, or perhaps of trout fishing in general. The fishing for speckles in the Adirondacks during the 1930s was clearly not what it had been a century or even a half century earlier. But it was still very good. My dad grew up in the heart of the Adirondacks, and he tells of grand brook trout fishing with his uncle in the ponds of Essex County during the '20s and '30s.

That all changed with the end of World War II and the building of roads and increased angling pressure. Once brook trout had disappeared from the ponds and lakes and rivers and streams—in fact, once American trout fishing in general had deteriorated significantly—the question of antibass sentiment would be another matter altogether.

For the moment the smallmouth bass had a number of important patrons and advocates, particularly in the Midwest. There, fly-fishing innovator Will Dilg began the Izaak Walton League. Dilg was an enthusiastic smallmouth angler, and one of the league's first acquisitions involved prime smallmouth habitat on the upper Mississippi River.

The Izaak Walton League boasted a membership of a hundred thousand in the mid-1920s. They weren't all smallmouth fishermen, of course. But enough of them were. Fly fishing for smallmouth bass was here to stay.

2 | *A Sport Nevertheless*

We can thank the waters of the midwest and mid-Atlantic regions for the tradition of fly fishing for smallmouths: the Ozark streams, the creeks and rivers of Kentucky, the Susqehanna and Potomac River watersheds, the waters of Illinois, Indiana, and Wisconsin—areas not suitable for trout, in other words. Here is where fly fishing for smallmouths has its roots.

Proximity to population centers meant that fly fishing for bass, if nothing else, was convenient. By the 1920s, trout fishing often meant a trek into the wilds; bass could be caught on the way home from work.

There was little exotic about smallmouth bass fishing. Trout flies had adventuresome connections with the waters that gave rise to their design—dry flies and the Catskills, streamers and Maine. Smallmouth flies were most often connected with their place of manufacture.

Standard smallmouth practice of the day called for gaudy wet flies. Next came Henshall's floating bass bug, with its clipped deer-hair body, bushy bucktail wings, and splayed tail. With the fly-rod tackle of the late nineteenth century, it must have cast about as well as a young robin.

But the bug caught bass—and plenty of fishermen, too.

Sometime around the turn of the century, cork-bodied bugs migrated north from their southern beginnings. The first commercial bug, named the Coaxer by its designer, William Jamison of Chicago, appeared around 1910. The Coaxer had a flat cork body and a pair of tail feathers that resembled the wings of popular wet flies.

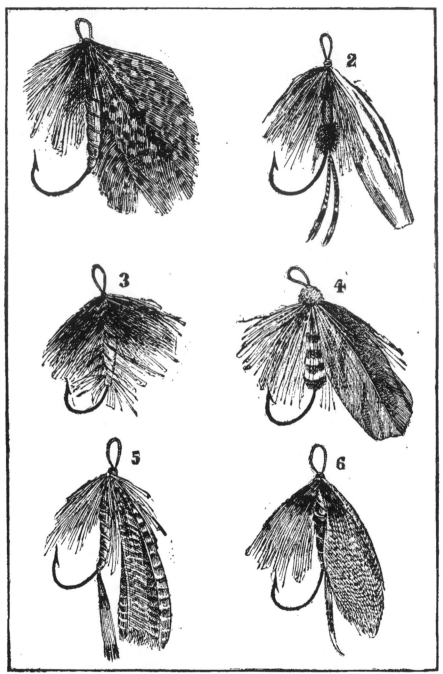

No. 1. Polka.   No. 2. Coachman.   No 3. Hackle.
No. 4. Bumble Bee.   No. 5. Abbey.   No. 6. Grizzly King.

Smallmouth flies of the nineteenth century followed the same prototypes of trout flies of the day.

A Henshall Bass Bug.

Several years later, a Tennessean named Ernest Peckinpaugh began selling his cork-bodied Night Bug. This pattern became the prototype of the standard cork-bodied popper. Then, as now, a good fly tyer needed some help from the press. Will Dilg, like Jamison, a Chicagoan, publicized Peckinpaugh's bug, and orders came pouring in from around the country.

Around the same time, Dilg and yet another Chicagoan, B. F. Wilder, collaborated on a bug of their own. It would be called the Wilder-Dilg or, more colloquially, the Feathered Minnow—the most popular bug of its day. The June 1922 issue of *National Sportsman,* for instance, had a back page advertising only bass bugs. Each had a different name, but an identical Wilder-Dilg arrangement of pointed cork head, hackle, and feathers. The page recalls that era's color plates of wet flies for trout—same pattern, different colors.

Sometime around 1920 another innovation in bass bugs appeared, this one thanks to deer hair. Whereas Henshall had flared and clipped the hair on his bug, Orley Tuttle, an angler from the trout-rich western Adirondacks, came up with a fly that featured the hair tied down over the hook. As Tony Atwill described in a 1979 *Fly Rod & Reel* article, Tuttle showed it to his wife, who exclaimed that it "looks like the Devil"; hence its name, Tuttle's Devil Bug.

Joe Messinger's hair frogs, with two-toned deer-hair bodies and kicking legs tied on at an angle, became popular in the 1930s. Other hair-and-cork patterns followed, and poppers and bugs came to dominate smallmouth fishing to an extent that dry flies never could with trout fishing. Such was the bass bug/popper's popularity that it may have limited the development of other smallmouth fishing techniques.

Ray Bergman, America's master angler of midcentury, told of a fishing trip in Vermont for smallmouth bass sometime in the 1930s. "Everyone," he wrote, "was fascinated with poppers." But the fishing was slow. He looked forward to his next stop, the St. Lawrence River.

He arrived to find that the bass were biting, but in deep water. Bergman, a fly fisherman first, decided to stick to his poppers and never touched a fish. Other boats came to the docks that night with "shimmering stringers of bass."

"Minnies," the guides replied when Bergman inquired about the bait.

"I decided that it was silly to have my foolish pride stand in the way of my fishing success," Bergman explained, "so I hired a guide and went with live bait." And he caught fish after fish on live shiners.

How interesting. The great pragmatic angler, the angler who triumphed time and again over perplexing on-the-stream situations, didn't think to try a sinking fly on these smallmouths.

And Bergman, in all fairness, wrote elsewhere of subsurface methods of bass fishing. Further, the St. Lawrence is a deep river. My point is certainly not to demean his angling skills but simply to indicate the poppers-or-nothing attitude that characterized the pre-World War II smallmouth scene.

Bass-fly innovations continued to involve deer hair. William Sturgis, in his 1940 book *Fly-Tying*, offered detailed instructions for tying a crayfish pattern. Of course, he used deer hair to tie it.

Bass flies, deer hair. Synonymous. Inseparable, even when crawled along the bottom.

Now, it isn't as if smallmouths woke up one day in 1985 and decided to start eating minnows, nymphs, and crustaceans. Some smallmouth anglers certainly did fish smallmouths with wet flies, streamers, and especially the spinner and fly.

And while midcentury fly fishing for smallmouths was hardly rife with innovations, neither was fly fishing for trout. But trout fishermen did have Bergman's *Trout* (1938) and, in particular, Preston Jennings's *Book of Trout Flies* (1935), which rested upon forage-based imitations. And there were other trout-fishing stirrings in this direction with the appearance of Art Flick's *Streamside Guide to Naturals and Their Imitations* (1947) and Ernest Schwiebert's *Matching the Hatch* (1955). In short, these books reflected a clear divergence of the ways we were coming to see bass and trout.

Trout were noble—no secret here. The more desired a quarry, the more desirable the qualities bestowed on it. With a sporting fish, that translated to qualities that made catching it challenging. Given their selectivity-based forage patterns, there was logic in conceiving of trout as wary, discriminating, and intelligent. Midcentury fly fishers hopped on this bus in a hurry.

With the popularity of the idea that bass of both species were ordinary came the supporting notion that they were pugnacious (they do fight hard!) and indiscriminating. Again, it fit perfectly with smallmouths' (and largemouths') opportunistic forage patterns. They were dumb and didn't know any better. How else to explain their ordinariness?

So the systematic, forage-based approach to fishing trout never got started with bass. There was neither interest in it nor a point to it. No doubt about it. In their souls, fly fishermen remained trout fishermen.

Then came the disastrous years following World War II. Brook trout underwent a serious decline because of increased fishing access and pressure. River fishing for

If brook trout proved unable to withstand the pressures of civilization, smallmouth bass were more than comfortable swimming in the shadow of industrialism.

browns and rainbows—yet to receive the boost it would from catch-and-release and environmentalism—deteriorated into a six-week put-and-take proposition.

Henshall was right about civilization and trout. But he was wrong about fly fishermen and bass. They missed their trout. With its British origins, fly fishing in America had always implied a certain class standing and a certain fish. This aesthetic, nurtured by the appearance of books praising trout, grew in potency as trout fishing's best days seemed to recede with each passing year.

If anything, the smallmouth's reputation among fly fishermen sank even lower during the 1950s. Whereas 1930s anglers like Victor Engels had no qualms about fishing for trout in the upper sections of Adirondack rivers and bass in the lower sections, the generation that followed grew increasingly edgy about bass in trout water. To feel otherwise, to replace brookies with bass, would have bordered on the sacrilegious.

This period marked the culmination of the same regional patterns that exist today, with antismallmouth sentiment strongest in northern New England, northern New York, and northern Michigan, last bastions of the brook trout.

To be sure, bass were not considered the same order of dangerous predator as the northern pike. Bass were viewed more as trash fish that somehow muscled trout out of the rivers, a behavior more benign than devouring them, as northerns were purported to do. Nobody shot smallmouths with deer rifles (as they do northern pike in Lake Champlain). But it was nothing to visit a river in trout country and find a pile of smallmouths drying in the sun.

In the end, smallmouths escaped the vilification that descended upon pike. Yet by escaping the strong feelings at one end of the continuum, they somehow never managed to excite them at the other. Often as not, their presence evoked a sort of resignation, best summed up in the oft-quoted remark Charles Waterman heard in 1970 from a Maine resort owner: "Oh bass are O.K., I guess. There's a fellow over in Portland who eats the damned things."

The rise and fall of a wonder fish is not exactly unheard of in fisheries management. The difference here is that smallmouth bass failed to live up to expectations that were social, not biological. Smallmouths held up well under the deteriorating environmental conditions. They thrived near population centers. They were aggressive. They preferred warm water to cold. They were adaptable.

In short, they *were* everything that Henshall had promised back in the nineteenth century. It was not the fish that changed in the intervening seventy-five years; it was the fisherman.

A lot of people went fishing during the postwar years, and most did so with spinning rods. The business side of the nascent fishing industry certainly recognized this trend: Whereas a 1922 edition of *Sports Afield* contained countless advertisements for trout flies and bass bugs, a 1953 edition had none—not a single one—for either.

Trout fishing's tradition was strong enough that the sport remained visible during this time, but what few smallmouth fly fishers there were seemed buried under the blizzard of silver, spools, and monofilament.

Spin and baitfishing for smallmouths became increasingly popular during the 1950s. A young Bob Clouser, whose Deep Minnow would revolutionize deep-water smallmouth fishing forty years down the road, waded the Susquehanna daily. He never saw another fly fisherman. Articles on smallmouth fly fishing usually (and understandably!) championed the smallmouth as a forgotten fish for fly anglers.

A number of writers got behind this one. William Blades's *Fishing Flies and Fly Tying*, published in 1951, included many patterns for smallmouths, including—remarkably enough—some that were forage-based, subsurface, and without a trace of deer hair.

So did *The Practical Fly Fisherman,* published in 1953. Author A. J. McClane, the influential fishing editor of *Field & Stream,* wrote of sophisticated smallmouths quite

River smallmouths feed on stonefly nymphs, though only recently have their imitations found acceptance with smallmouth anglers.

unlike the bass of fifty years earlier. In those days, an angler could easily get along with four or five wet flies. Modern smallmouth fishing was different. "Any fly can be called a bass fly," he noted, "but not all flies are good bass flies." McClane, in fact, used nymphs to catch smallmouths.

Other fishing writers—Jason Lucas, John Alden Knight, Joe Brooks, Ted Trueblood—began to write with enthusiasm of bass bugging. McClane's colleague at *Field & Stream*, H. G. Tapply, the great New England writer, wrote with enthusiasm about light-tackle bass bugging and fly fishing for smallmouths in rivers, noting that ". . . river smallmouths are heavy nymph feeders, and at times lake fish feast on them too.

"If you stop to think of it," he concluded, "trout wouldn't be held in such high regard if most of them were caught on plug casting tackle."

Heresy in the heart of brook trout country.

As Waterman, Schullery, and others have noted, however, care must be taken when inferring any kind of larger angling consensus from a period's written material. Writers of the 1950s and '60s may have enthusiastically articulated the pleasures of fishing

Traditionally, a bass was a bass. It's only in the last couple of decades that anglers have made an effort to distinguish between a largemouth and a smallmouth.

for smallmouths, but their fly-fishing readers had already promised their hearts to the brookies, browns, rainbows, cutthroats, landlocks, and Atlantics. This is key to understanding the status of smallmouth bass in the fly-fishing community—then and now.

It should also be noted that, throughout the period, little distinction was made between smallmouths and largemouths. Bass were bass. Most writers lumped the species

With improving water quality in the lower stretches of rivers, fly fishers began to realize the virtues of fishing for wild bass rather than 8-inch stocked trout.

together under "Black Bass," with largemouth tactics the currency—even when small-mouths were the quarry. For instance, McClane's fly list, explicit and carefully considered, clearly recognized the increasing "sophistication" of black bass—even if it overlooked the detail that two different species were involved.

In a sense this is understandable. Fly fishers are used to various species of trout sharing a feeding riffle. The various species of black bass, however, have little interest in family picnics.

Things changed in the 1970s. Increasing numbers of fly fishers looked to horizons beyond deteriorating trout fishing, and one of them had smallmouths on it. The improving nature of tackle, together with the modification of fly-fishing methods for new species, meant that fly fishing for smallmouths was entering a new era.

Bob Clouser reports that fly fishers began appearing on the Susquehanna during this time. Numbers increased on the Potomac and the Delaware, too. The large rivers of the midwestern and western United States; the springtime shallows of north country ponds, reservoirs, and lakes; the lower sections of trout streams everywhere—all became places to fly fish for smallmouth bass. They were close to home, often on the outskirts of town, but they offered a refreshing experience: It was possible to fish whenever you wanted, see no one, and catch spring-tailed wild fish until you tired of it. The experience harked back to another time, to fly fishing for trout a century earlier—ironically enough, often in the very same waters.

Meanwhile, interest in forage-based fly fishing grew with the publication of books such as *Selective Trout* and *Hatches,* and spread beyond trout to other species. It was only a matter of time before the fly-fishing world discovered that smallmouths could be caught more readily with tactics designed just for them and not with largemouths in mind. Writers like Lefty Kreh, Charles Waterman, and Dave Whitlock began writing with insight about smallmouth techniques and with enthusiasm about smallmouth sport.

In the 1980s, articles on subsurface fishing for smallmouths began appearing (along with popper and bug articles, of course) in the various fly-fishing magazines. Pictures of largemouth bass, often as not, accompanied these articles. I guess the largemouths were bigger.

By the late 1980s photo editors began to get the species right, though the pictures still left something to be desired. One notable attempt involved a full-page color photo of an angler landing an obviously mounted smallmouth. (One can imagine the howl that might have arisen over a stuffed brookie.)

In 1989, Harry Murray published *Fly Fishing for Smallmouth Bass,* the first and only book devoted exclusively to fly fishing for smallmouths. Murray focused on forage-based imitation, on reading smallmouth streams and rivers, and on presenting flies in a lifelike manner. *Fly Fishing for Smallmouth Bass* remains an invaluable guide to fishing moving flows.

Most recently, Bob Clouser's Deep Minnow has been a driving force behind smallmouth fishing's expansion to deeper waters. Various crayfish, hellgrammite, and sculpin imitations have appeared as well. Equipped with fast-sink lines and graphite rods, increasing numbers of fly fishers are drawn to reservoirs and lakes, and not just during spawning time, as in the past.

In short, fly fishing for smallmouths is getting a second look these days—still not with the passion of trout or salmon fishing or the fever inspired by salt water, but a sec-

The Clouser Minnow opened up deep-water fly fishing for smallmouths.

ond look nevertheless. With the improving water quality of the nation's lakes and rivers, there have never been more smallmouths. And with the growing interest in fly fishing, there have never been more fly fishers looking for something to catch.

Smallmouth fishing in the 1990s retains its regional flavor. Harry Murray runs a school on the Shenandoah. Outfitters driftfish on the New River in West Virginia. The Boundary Waters of Minnesota draw numerous surface addicts. Bob Clouser, the famous fly designer and guide on the Susquehanna, is booked every day for a year ahead. Dave Wolff, another guide on the Susquehanna, tells of increasing numbers of anglers who book for trout and end up fishing for smallmouths.

At the same time, many Maine anglers ignore smallmouths to fish for the new "hot" fish, the striped bass. In Vermont, a recent survey placed smallmouths fifth in a list of favorite fish behind brookies, browns, rainbows, and yellow perch. (Interestingly, non-

The frontiers of fly fishing for smallmouths seem to be expanding all the time.

residents ranked smallmouths second behind brook trout!) I have a tough time getting anybody to go smallmouth fishing with me here in New England—except in July. For these fly fishers there is interest, yes, enthusiasm at times, but seldom passion.

I grew up along the bass-rich shores of Lake Ontario and the St. Lawrence River. At least three towns call themselves the "Home of the Black Bass," and I've never heard anyone ask which kind. Here there is a passion for smallmouths.

Fly fishing for them remains another matter, and in the years I've fished the lake and the river I've never seen another fly fisher—except for those fishing with me.

Last year I was unable to get back for opening day, the third Saturday in June. When I did make it up there a week later, Jack LaHare—a truly whacked bass fisherman— explained that the fishing had been good despite windy, rough conditions on the lake.

"Windy as hell," Jack said. "Almost couldn't get out." He'd been fishing at Hard- scrabble Bay on eastern Lake Ontario. Big water.

"A lot of boats?"

"Packed," Jack said. "You could walk across 'em. Hey, there were some fly fish- ermen, too. Like you. They were unbelievable. Sitting in inner tubes, flailing away into the wind. But they caught some bass."

"Good," I said. "Good for them."

3

The Biological Bass

E ven though smallmouths have become an increasingly popular item in the fly-fishing press, their biology and life cycle receive little attention. No tomes here. Bass behavior? Well, let's see. They spawn in the spring, guard their nests, and basically clobber anything that comes within sight.

Beyond that, smallmouth behavior remains a shadowy affair.

HABITAT

Clear-water lakes, ponds, flows, and rivers provide the best habitat. Smallmouths have also done well in reservoirs and tailraces, and the country's largest specimens swim in these waters in the upper South. In 1955, Dale Hollow Lake in Tennessee produced the world-record smallmouth, an 11-pound 5-ounce beauty. (The largest smallmouth taken on a fly rod came from Washington's Columbia River in 1966 and tipped the scales at 8 pounds 12 ounces.)

Smallmouths also do well in rather turbid streams—so long as gravel and/or rock form the stream bottom. Given the importance of sculpins, darters, and crayfish in smallmouths' diets, such a substrate is virtually imperative. Weeds are an important ingredient in any smallmouth habitat, too, as the grass provides cover for smaller bass and baitfish.

Studies indicate that smallmouths do best in lakes with a maximum depth of at least 30 feet. Escaping warm water seems less the issue than avoiding competition with largemouths.

Smallmouths thrive in riverine environments. The country's largest and longest river systems comprise our classic smallmouth waters. Smallmouths also do well in the lower stretches of trout streams, where the water quality may be good but the temperature is excessive for trout. Smallmouths, it turns out, can tolerate water temperatures through the 70s and even into the low 80s, although they prefer them in the 60s.

SURVIVAL/MORTALITY

Smallmouth bass begin life as fertilized eggs approximately 1/10 inch in diameter. The eggs eventually hatch into tiny fish less than 1/5 inch long. The fry hide in the rocks for a few days, living off their yolk sacs, before venturing forth totally black (hence the name "black bass"). They remain so for a couple weeks, swarming around with their mouths open, swallowing whatever happens to drift in.

A male smallmouth guarding the nest.

Like any small creatures, the fry face heavy predation. But because a single nest can produce up to ten thousand tiny bass, the predation does more good than harm. Weather is a different story. Heavy flooding of a stream or river can result in the loss of an entire age class. The resulting turbidity disorients the tiny fish—they use light or its absence to find their way around—and heavy flows simply wash them into the main currents and downstream into oblivion.

In reservoirs, lakes, and ponds, water temperature is often the deciding factor in the survival of a year class. Some studies show that low temperature during midsummer undercuts the survival rates of the fry, presumably by limiting the overall productivity of the water; other studies, such as one conducted on Oneida Lake in New York, identify June (spawning season there) weather as the key factor—the hotter the month, the higher the survival rate. Still other studies emphasize the importance of smallmouths reaching 6 centimeters by the end of their first summer; otherwise they are likely to starve during the winter months.

Smallmouths reach sexual maturity in the third or fourth year, with later maturation in some waters. The maximum age for the species is about fifteen years, though a fish of that age is rare. In general, the harsh climate that characterizes much of the smallmouth's range means that 45 to 60 percent of the *adult* bass in any water fail to survive from one year to the next. First-year spawners—those in the 12- to 14-inch range—appear most susceptible to winter mortality.

Catch-and-release, then, becomes an interesting question. Traditional angler harvest has little effect in some situations. The smallmouth bass fishery in eastern Lake Ontario is a good example. "At present time," notes Al Schiavone, fisheries biologist with the New York State Department of Environmental Conservation, "evidence suggests that smallmouth year classes fluctuate based on the weather. There is no evidence that angler harvest hurts the total survival of the population [the number of fish that survive from year to year]."

Other research finds catch-and-release crucial to the well-being of a fishery. More big smallmouths leaves more fish surviving winter starvation and ultimately more return spawners. Mark Ridgway's work in Ontario's Algonquin Park emphasizes the importance of adults spawning at a large size, finding that the high mortality rate of smaller spawners can make a significant difference in the overall age structure in a given water.

A concentration of anglers in an area can make releasing fish important, not just on smaller waters but on sections of bigger ones as well. And on southern waters, where year-to-year survival rates may be greater, catch-and-release is vital to improving a fishery. The Susquehanna River, for instance, has sustained a good deal of pressure over the years. With the growth of catch-and-release, more and more of the fish taken are now released, and the average size of the fish has increased substantially. Bob Clouser notes a marked improvement in the fishing on the Susquehanna below Harrisburg since a 15-inch minimum size was introduced.

SEASONS

Ridgway's research in Algonquin Provincial Park indicates that bass use different sections of a lake during spawning, summer, and winter. They tend to remain identified with one section for each season.

Early in the summer, smallmouths recuperate from the rigors of spawning by schooling loosely along weedy drop-offs, rocky shorelines, boulder/weedy areas, and

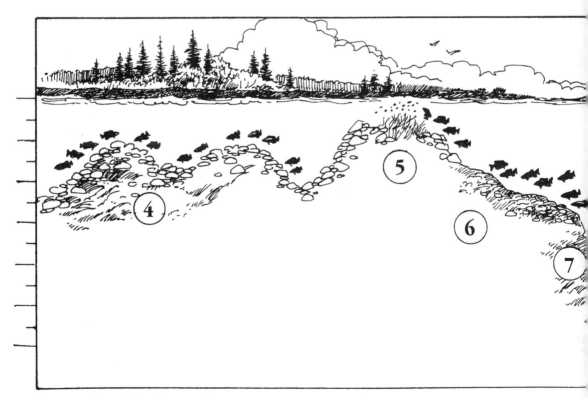

A smallmouth lake in spring, summer, and fall. Key: (1) pre-spawn (2) spawn (3) post-spawn (4) summer (5) late summer (6) early fall (7) mid fall (8) late fall (9) winter.

gravel shoals. Even in the deepest lakes, postspawn finds smallmouths in fairly shallow waters, under 15 feet.

As the summer builds, smallmouths forage along productive structures. They have fairly large home ranges, as large as 400 to 600 acres. Researchers in the Algonquin Park study found them constantly associated with other bass and covering up to 7 miles per day.

Other studies on smaller lakes suggest less movement, smaller home ranges. Those studies focusing on smaller rivers emphasize the smallmouth's homebody nature. It turns out that some fish stay in the same large pool throughout the summer season.

Smallmouths leave their summer ranges in the fall. Schools concentrate, moving deeper as the water cools. With the onset of cold weather in late fall, smallmouths arrive at wintering areas and remain there, assuming a state of semihibernation beneath the winter ice.

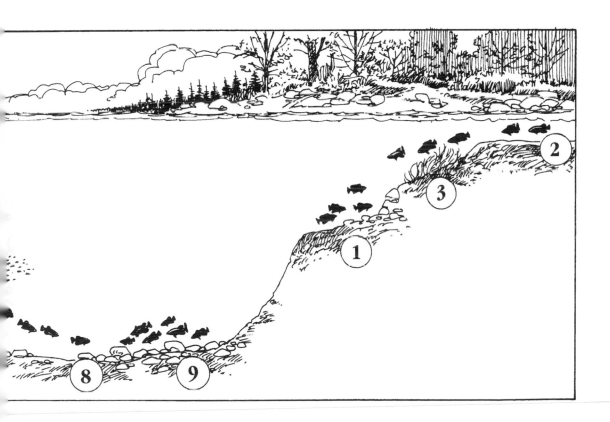

In lakes they school tightly, gathering over flat bottoms. In rivers they drift to the deepest holes and may actually enter the crevices of rocks and ledges. In the words of one scientific paper, "In streams, rough substrate to brace against or protect from the current is necessary to prevent downstream displacement of the inactive fish." Sound sleepers, in other words.

The males approach prespawn staging areas when lakes open up in the spring. As temperatures edge through the 50s, they look for protected areas of gravel and rubble that could make suitable spots for spawning. Smallmouths occasionally spawn on clay or silty bottoms, but generally prefer rocky or gravel substrate. River bass spawn in areas protected from the main flow; lake fish spawn in either tributaries or bays, usually in depths of 4–12 feet.

Once the water temperature nears 60 degrees, smallmouths move into spawning bays. Males build nests, then females appear on the scene. They come closer and closer to the nests, nudged in that direction by males. Spawning occurs when a female releases her eggs over a nest and a male simultaneously fertilizes them.

The male then guards the nest from intruders—fiercely. Certain species of darters lay their own eggs near smallmouth nests and thereby enjoy the benefit of the male's vigilance. For the record, things change pretty quickly once his child care duties conclude. He'd as soon eat his progeny as look at them.

A HEALTHY, HAPPY APPETITE

During their first two years, smallmouths feed almost exclusively on insects. Beginning with the third year—at which time they may well be 7 to 8 inches in length—their diet shifts to bigger forage, such as leeches, crayfish, frogs (including tadpoles), and baitfish.

The shift can be quite dramatic. Studies indicate that aquatic insects make up 95 percent of the forage of young-of-the-year bass and nearly 90 percent of that of second-year bass. After that, insects make up from 0–5 percent, with some variation.

At times, adult smallmouths do take aquatic insects, particularly in streams and rivers. Stoneflies, mayflies, and caddis are probably the most important menu items. In one study, bass beneath a section of heavy rapids fed heavily on caddis flies. The authors speculated that the drowned caddis arrived via the waterfall and made for easy pickings, which the bass took readily. Smallmouths in other sections of the same stream, where caddis were present but not concentrated, took them only incidentally.

Although juvenile smallmouths feed heavily on smaller aquatic nymphs, adult fish prefer a bigger meal.

A similar pattern characterizes smallmouth feeding in general. That is, smallmouths tend to feed on the forage that is most abundant and most available. Smallmouths in one lake in Canada, for instance, even fed heavily on plankton!

None of which means that we should be tying size-28 flies with pea-green floss. Indeed, whereas smallmouths often eat the most common forage, they remain consummate opportunists.

A fascinating study conducted on Bull Shoals Reservoir in Arkansas exemplifies this point. Smallmouth stomach samples revealed few crayfish during spring, summer, and fall, when crayfish are typically a preferred forage. On this lake crayfish became the dominant forage during midwinter.

This peculiar seasonal pattern was explained by the fact that the crayfish lived in "large, blocky, angular chert." They could escape by slipping between the rocks—except during the winter when the cold water slowed down their metabolisms, allowing the smallmouths to catch them.

As the water warmed in the spring, the smallmouths continued to hunt crayfish, with less success. It just so happened, however, that the windswept, rocky shoreline provided excellent habitat for *Stenonema* mayfly nymphs, of all things, which began hatching with the warming of the water. This activity did not go unnoticed by the bass, evidently, and as the study noted, "*Stenonema* sp. were consumed in large numbers by adult smallmouths."

Abundant *and* available, in other words. Here and elsewhere, smallmouths are always quick to switch from selectivity to opportunism when something better comes along. It may be best to refer to them (and a number of researchers have) as just that: selective opportunists, always quick to take choice baits that may not be part of their standard fare. A number of writers, for example, have noted the tendency of larger smallmouths to feed on hatching insects, then turn to chubs midway through the hatch when these larger forage become available.

Some types of forage don't even have to be abundant and available to get a smallmouth's attention. Frogs come to mind here. Very few smallmouths subsist on a frogs-only diet; at the same time, if the fish are hunting for food in shallow water few are going to pass one up, either, even if they've been chomping down chubs all week. Popper fishermen are eternally grateful.

Smallmouths often do end up feeding exclusively on a preferred forage, a behavior probably more common on big or fertile waters capable of producing a substantial volume of a particular forage—enough to sustain regular predation. Put another way, larger, productive waters may demand less opportunism on the part of resident smallmouths and in the end permit more selectivity.

Smallmouths hunting crayfish along an acre-wide shoal on a fertile lake, for instance, probably have all the eating they can handle right in front of them; they can ignore a school of perch swimming over their heads. Smallmouths holding in a stream eddy simply may not have the luxury of such selectivity. (A similar analogy can be drawn between a pig-fat brown trout on the Bighorn and an 8-inch brook trout in a mountain stream.)

Actual feeding behavior varies with water type. In general, the smaller the water the more likely smallmouths will be to use cover. In rivers, smallmouths hold in fertile areas or move into rocky areas that offer current breaks and hence attract forage, such as minnows, crayfish, or large aquatic nymphs. In small lakes, smallmouths may move less each day, perhaps only from deep to shallow water at dawn and dusk. There does seem to be less daily movement in fertile waters. In larger lakes, smallmouths may take

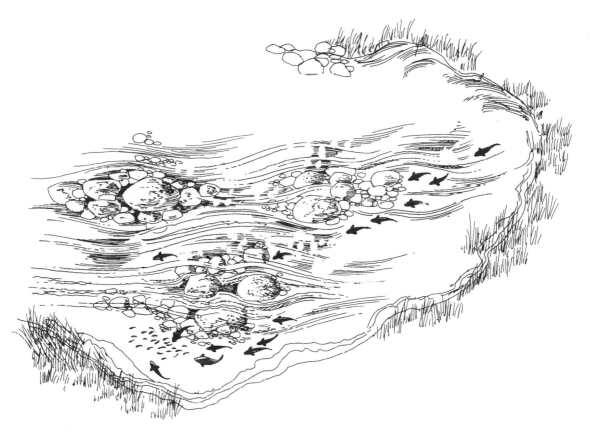

A school of smallmouths, seen from above, moving from one shoal on to the next, "running their trapline" for forage.

what Ontario biologist Mark Ridgway calls a "trapline approach" to foraging: They follow the same route over and over in their search for open-water baitfish or crayfish.

Smallmouths swim in schools during summer and fall, with juveniles and adults in different groups because of their different forage requirements. This schooling behavior helps bass forage more efficiently, though it's not clear exactly why. They wouldn't forage in schools, however, unless it offered some advantage. (See chapters 9 and 10 for more on this behavior.)

The preferred forage varies with the season. During spring and early summer it's likely to be baitfish. Darters, sculpins, shiners, minnows, shad, dace, chubs, and alewives are particularly popular. Smallmouths often exercise their opportunistic nature by going from species to species of baitfish. In lieu of substantial populations of crayfish and baitfish, juvenile panfish and gamefish are popular food items, too.

Smallmouths in different sections of a lake feed in different ways at the same moment. Here a school of smallmouths in the shallows feeds on shiners, while another school in deeper water feeds on crayfish.

In some larger southern waters, bigger smallmouths may stay with forage fish all summer long. Other lakes and rivers with less substantial populations of baitfish and heavier populations of crayfish are a different matter. And finally, as researcher Steve Quinn notes in reference to a Lake Ontario study, both can be true: "A study of small-mouths living in a bay of Lake Ontario found that some adults fed pelagically on alewives and other prey over sandy areas with little cover. Another group of more sedentary bass inhabited rocky shoals and fed primarily on bottom-dwelling crayfish and other invertebrates. In waters with more complex types of habitat and various prey, fish of all sizes more likely adopt different movement and feeding patterns. . . ."

So the next time someone starts telling you "what the bass are doing," there's only one response: Which ones?

Despite individual differences, however, some foraging patterns emerge. Typically, smallmouths focus on baitfish during the spring and fall and favor crayfish during the warm-weather months, when they "hatch."

Although smallmouths become opportunists when feeding on insects and baitfish, they lean toward selectivity when it comes to crayfish. They prefer smaller specimens, which some researchers attribute to the fact that small crayfish are the most common forage (most abundant) and are easier to handle (more available) than larger crayfish. (See chapter 10 for a full discussion of crayfish).

As crayfish become less available (i.e., molting ends) during the fall, and as young-of-the-year baitfish grow in size (in essence becoming more abundant), smallmouths return to baitfish as their chief forage. And they often move some distance to find them, sometimes into very shallow water.

One steamy August afternoon several years ago, my wife, Noreen, and I were sloshing along a sandy beach on Lake Ontario, about to go for a swim. It had been very hot, and the shallows were warm. "Like bathwater," Noreen said.

Clusters of shiners darted ahead of us, glinting in the sun. They milled beneath the roots of a shoreline willow, where the waves had worn a depression. I waded over to scatter them and received quite a start when several smallmouth bass came flying out of there along with the minnows. Late-summer smallmouths can be found in *very* shallow water.

Summer in general is a time for smallmouths to expand their home range; with the cooling water of fall comes a contraction. This is a crucial time for smallmouths. They follow forage more intensely in fall than at any other time of the year. The amount of forage they pack away, the amount of energy they conserve—*that* dictates whether they survive the winter starvation and spring spawning. Everybody wants seconds.

Smallmouths feed on baitfish through the fall. They remain active as long as the temperature lingers in the low 60s and upper 50s. Below 50, feeding slows to a crawl.

Sweet dreams.

4 Principles of Smallmouth Fishing

I 'm sure there are people around who know a lot more about fly fishing for smallmouth bass than I do. I'll bet they've hooked and landed bigger fish, and more of them, and are, in general, better at it. No doubt.

But nobody I know has spent a bigger chunk of childhood trying to figure out how to catch one. Growing up during the 1950s I encountered my share of secret lures, gizmos, and other technological wonders of the modern age. It was hard not to be suckered—still is, for that matter. At age seven I was convinced I'd found the perfect lure. It would bring me some big trout in the spring, yes. More importantly, it would definitely result in my first smallmouth bass. Ah! Dreams of youth.

The object of my affection was a French lure with a motorized tail. It was called a Vivif, and an enterprising sales clerk had set it up in a tank so that it swam around and around. Every day after school, me and my friends would charge through the gray March afternoon into the store, fly down the aisles into Sporting Goods. There we'd encircle the tank, watching the lure. Cats on a goldfish.

We debated its merits, saved our money. My friend Lee thought the batteries would get wet; I thought we'd have all the fish we'd need by that point, so who would give a damn. We finally got the money together to buy one—we'd decided we'd take turns using it—and walked into the department store with some business to take care of.

After school at the Vivif tank.

We got to Sporting Goods. The tank was drained.

"Sold the last one this morning," the clerk said, dismantling the exhibit. "And there won't be any more."

The fish I could have caught.

* * *

So I've always been pretty serious about fishing, even when I was a kid. Trout, bullheads, and panfish—that's what I caught, mostly. Somehow I got hooked on the idea of bass, though, which was strange because my opportunities for catching them were limited.

Not by geography. I grew up in Watertown, New York, less than twenty minutes from the great smallmouth fishing in Lake Ontario and the St. Lawrence River. But as a small boy, I had a tough time finding anybody who would take me.

My dad, born and raised in the Adirondack Mountains, was a dedicated trout fisherman, quite oblivious to our proximity to smallmouths. I looked west to the broad expanses of the Great Lakes, but he looked east to the balsam forests and spruce swamps of the Adirondacks. Not that I minded; I liked trout fishing just fine. We went every weekend, and the last thing I wanted was to be left behind.

But I also pined to go bass fishing, an activity my father put into the category of things you did when you had the garden weeded. Here I was in the middle of the smallmouth fishing capital of the Northeast and I couldn't get my hands on them.

It was my good fortune that my dad was a schoolteacher, which meant that he worked at summer jobs, such as they were. He somehow ended up in the fast-paced world of the Thousand Island State Park Commission as a toll booth attendant.

That's really how I got started catching smallmouths—on the St. Lawrence River. I didn't have a clue what I was doing and caught only an occasional undersized smallmouth by accident when fishing off the docks. But then my dad got me hooked up with his friend Don Wolfe, the park caretaker, the area's best smallmouth fisherman.

Don was a strange bird—tall, sinewy, tough as a shoreline cedar. He lived his life on the river, and it was as if the winds and currents and stony shores had fashioned his very being. He had a small head and long, anvil arms. Poor eyesight gave him a flinty look, even when driving the garbage truck in the morning.

Don would do anything for people he liked and nothing for everyone else. Carving prizewinning decoys, photographing wildlife, raising Great Danes, and hunting waterfowl, brant in particular—those were his passions. Those, and smallmouth fishing.

Don liked my dad, which explained his interest in my smallmouth fishing development. He certainly didn't have much use for the other fishermen in the park, calling them tourists and even worse in private.

I remember meeting him next to the park dumptruck one hot and dusty August noon hour.

My dad said, "Don, do you suppose you could explain to my son here how to catch a bass? He's been trying all summer, and he'd like to catch a couple before he has to go back to school."

Don gave me the once-over, like he was trying to decide whether to lend me money.

"Get yourself some shiners, and go up to the head of Linda Island," he said, as he stepped around in back of the truck and pointed out to the river, which showed in bright blue patches through the trees. "You can see it right there."

"Well that's where he's been going, Don," my dad said, then looked at me. "Isn't it?"

"Yup," I nodded.

"What do you do," my dad asked, "drift the shiners?"

"You just let your boat float along with the current. Hook the shiner through the lips and drift it right along the bottom. You should feel the split shot rapping on the rocks."

"I been anchoring. When I try drifting, I keep catching weeds."

"You fishing inside the island or outside?"

"Inside."

Don Wolfe (right) with tourist, circa 1961.

"It's pretty shallow in there. The bass are a little deeper right now, closer to twenty or twenty-five feet. If you see bottom or keep on getting weeds, you're too shallow. Try the outside of the island and put on enough split shot to get it below the rock bass.

"If you keep getting hung up, take a split shot off; if you don't feel bottom, put one on." He looked at me like he'd forgotten something. "Know what to do when a bass bites?"

"Let him take it."

"Let him take it good."

With the world set right, Don climbed back up in his truck and started the engine. "Thanks, Don," my dad said.

"Yeah, thanks, Don," I added.

The next morning I got my bait and headed out to the island. Once there, I grabbed a minnow, hooked it through the lips as I'd been instructed, and drifted along, split shot tapping on the rocks. The rod tip bent down sharply, then sprang back. I hurried it in to find a bare hook. A fish!

I baited up with another minnow and dropped it overboard. Something grabbed it with a feel different from the sharp pecks of panfish. This was a thump, an I-mean-business-mister kind of thump, and when it came again, I leaned back on that glass rod for all I was worth. The monofilament rose through the green water. A bass twisted toward the sky, spraying water, and I held on.

Near the boat, the fish swirled at the top, disgorging minnows, some still twitching.

Gulls came squawking down out of the heavens, swooping after the baitfish. My line sawed through the water.

And my mind raced with visions of fishing glory to come.

* * *

There's a good deal of interest in smallmouths these days. If numbers of national-magazine articles are any indication, smallmouth bass have become the third or fourth most popular freshwater fish in the country, behind largemouths and walleyes, about even with trout, and ahead of crappies, catfish, and pike.

Fishing for smallmouths used to be a local art based on experience and intuition, but in recent years it has become more scientific and analytical, thanks to a proliferation of media coverage and, most of all, the rise of professional bass fishing. Smallmouths aren't as popular as largemouths, but a good number of big-time professional tournaments have been won because one guy found the smallmouths and nobody else could.

Nevertheless, the essence of smallmouth fishing remains largely the same as it was in the days of Don Wolfe. Much of what he explained to me that noon hour thirty-five years ago and much of what I did in response would work today: Find the fish, and make a natural presentation with an appealing bait, lure, or fly. Put it right in front of them. If something works once, keep doing it.

Fly fishers can learn a great deal, not only from the legacies of the Don Wolfes of the smallmouth world, but from the techniques developed by professional fishers. Today's angler certainly has access to information on how to catch smallmouths.

In general, fishing principles emerge from the biology, starting with the idea that smallmouth location, behavior, and forage change from season to season. At first glance, spin and baitfishing may seem far removed from the self-conscious world of postmodern fly fishing. In fact, today's fly fishers stand to learn a great deal from the humble practitioners of glitter and grime.

SEASONAL PATTERNS: Principle #1

Nowadays anglers fish for smallmouths twelve months a year. Winter fishing in the southern part of the country produces the biggest fish, usually prespawn females. These fish are often taken on offshore humps during the early winter and, as spring approaches, in deep water near spawning areas.

Farther north, anglers catch some winter bass in warm-water releases in major rivers. Otherwise, pickings are slim. I once caught a smallmouth on a minnow on December 17 in the Deerfield River in Massachusetts. The fish was 10 inches long and the water temperature was 42 degrees. This was before I realized that smallmouth got washed into crevices during the winter months. I would read with skepticism any magazine articles about winter fly fishing for smallmouths.

With the coming of spring, smallmouths rediscover their appetites. Live minnows and their imitations are the order of the day. Early spring presents a good opportunity to catch a trophy, as prespawn females often can be located on the outside edges of spawning areas.

As water temperatures reach the upper 50s, the bass move on to gravel spawning areas. Virtually any technique, from working poppers to working jigs, fly fishing to bait casting, can work. But that changes as the females drift off to recuperate from spawning, leaving smaller males guarding the nests. The fishing for them gradually tails off, too.

Summer smallmouth fishing starts slowly. In fact, the early summer or postspawn period has a reputation for providing the poorest fishing of the season. Recuperating bass scatter along shorelines. They can be tough to find, tougher to catch. Popular strategies include trolling plugs, casting spinners and spinner baits, and drifting live bait.

As summer builds, fish regroup, foraging routes develop, and better fishing results. A variety of smallmouth methods produce during midsummer, from "trout-stream" tactics in smaller rivers to "largemouth-surface" tactics at dusk and dawn in ponds and flows. Canoe anglers float-fish rivers, and big-water anglers probe the depths with live bait, jigs, and deep-running crankbaits. They all catch their share of fish. Summertime and the living is easy.

Autumn fishing can be exceptional. September brings a profusion of bait, not to mention smallmouths looking to put on some weight for the winter. October and early November often feature flurries of activity, particularly in deeper water. But as the water temperature falls into the 50s the fishing slows. Once it hits 50 degrees, the fishing ends for the season in most areas.

Each year, lake trout anglers catch many big, pre-spawn smallmouths by fishing shiners on the bottom right at ice-out.

STRUCTURED SMALLMOUTHS: Principle #2

The second principle of smallmouth fishing involves their nearly constant orientation to a structure.

"Structure" means a transition in bottom type or depth of water. In streams it can be nothing more than a boulder, the lip of a pool, or a deep shoreline. In smaller lakes and ponds, deep shorelines, brushpiles, and blowdowns constitute important structures. (As noted earlier, fish in small waters—ponds and streams—often hang closer to cover.) Weed beds and offshore humps and shoals are key points on lakes and reservoirs.

The relationship of smallmouths to structure is a constant. Weeds, rocks/boulders, and blowdowns all provide good foraging for hungry smallmouths.

Smallmouths hold close to the bottom or substrate in shallow water, too. That's where their forage lives. There are some exceptions—fish in summer rivers feeding on insects, for one; fish in big lakes feeding on open-water baitfish, for another.

Experienced smallmouth anglers intuitively match approach to water depth and structure. Shallow water and weeds requires a horizontal presentation, i.e., spinners, crankbaits, surface lures; deeper water and rock calls for a vertical presentation, i.e., jigs and live bait.

NOT AS DUMB AS YOU THINK: Principle #3

Smallmouth bass get wise to fishing pressure. Smallmouths that don't get fished much are often interested in topwater plugs—particularly in shallow and weedy areas of rivers. Those that encounter a fair amount of pressure, on the other hand, seem most likely to take a tube jig or live bait near the bottom.

Regardless of method, the first few casts or drifts often draw a strike from the biggest active bass on the shoal or in the spot. Perhaps big bass get first crack at what-

ever food appears and smaller fish get what's left—whether that means a suspicious morsel, or any morsel during a cold front, when the bigger fish don't feel like eating.

One study found that as northern pike were caught and released, they came to refuse artificial lures but continued to strike live bait at the same rate. The same principle appears to apply to a school of bass. They don't turn down a well-presented bait, but do grow increasingly skeptical of flies and artificials (tube jigs tend to hold appeal longest, though not to the extent of live bait). Eventually the only customers will be smaller and smaller bass that really can't afford to pass up any opportunity to eat. Changing lures or flies might fool a fish or two, but that action also tails off, more quickly each time. What remains of the school moves on. With the shoal area free of large predators, rock bass and perch move in—until the next school of smallmouths makes its appearance.

Smallmouths wise up with fishing pressure.

WHEN TO FISH: Principle #4

Smallmouths are civilized fish. They feed throughout the day, although dawn and dusk remain top times. They are nowhere near the night feeders that largemouths are, although smallmouths in southern waters may be more nocturnal than those in waters to the north. And under the cover of darkness, topwater noisemakers can produce some good fish in clear-water ponds and lakes that get a lot of fishing pressure and boat traffic. My friend Ted Creighton took a nocturnal 6-pounder from just such a water in Connecticut; before dark the boat wakes had made fishing on the surface impossible.

Most anglers agree that smallmouths (like other fish) are most active in the hours before a front hits and less active in the several days after it goes through. All in all, stable weather patterns bring the most predictable fishing, and the influence of weather seems most pronounced on bigger waters.

LARGEMOUTHS, NOT: Principle #5

About smallmouths and largemouths, H. G. Tapply once wrote, "Aside from a family resemblance and a quarrelsome nature, they really don't have much in common." Largemouths generally prefer heavily weeded or wooded waters that permit them to ambush baitfish. Although they may move to considerable depths in certain clear-water reservoirs, they prefer lakes that feature heavy vegetation, slack current, and water less than 10 feet deep.

Very few good largemouth lakes are also good smallmouth lakes—unless the water is big enough to include the range of habitats that will accommodate the very different needs of both species. Smallmouths and largemouths do share habitat in smaller waters occasionally. But sooner or later (and usually sooner) the habitat begins to favor one species or the other.

Largemouths and smallmouths look somewhat alike, and that has blurred their behavioral differences. As noted earlier, "bass" has always implied largemouths, not smallmouths; lily pads and stumps, not rocky shoals; jitterbugs, not jigs; frogs, not crayfish.

It's understandable. While smallmouths are different from trout, trout fishing methods *work* for them. Moreover, smallmouths sometimes share habitat with trout.

Largemouths don't, though. They live in snake-filled swamps, inhale fist-sized poppers and bugs, and have obscene bellies that threaten to split their skins. Under the cover of darkness, you're never sure whether a splash comes from a rising bigmouth or a stumbling heifer. The fishing, in other words, is so different from trout fishing that it is its own thing: bass fishing.

So for years, smallmouth fishing followed largemouth dictum, with heavy line and big lures designed for shallow-water fishing in heavy cover. But in recent years that has changed, and people are realizing that the more they understand smallmouths independently from largemouths (and trout, for that matter), the more angling success they will enjoy.

Crayfish make excellent live bait for summer smallmouths.

BEST BAITS: Principle #6

These days increasing numbers of smallmouth anglers use smaller lures and jigs and lines in the 2- to 8-pound class. The lighter lines permit fishing smaller lures closer to the bottom with some sensitivity. In general, the deeper the fishing, the smaller the lure or bait.

Live bait is the surest way to catch smallmouths, and it probably accounts for more fish than any other method. Three types are the most important: shiners, particularly early and late in the season; crayfish, most notably between mid-July and mid-September; and hellgrammites, especially in rivers.

Leeches and polliwogs are two offbeat "localized" baits. Night crawlers often produce when they're least expected to, and live crickets can be terrific in late summer in small lakes and ponds. A bait doesn't have to occur indigenously to keep bass coming. My old fishing buddy Pete Bellinger and I once caught bass after bass on live hellgrammites in the Chaumont Bay section of Lake Ontario. Those bass had never seen a hellgrammite in their lives.

BEST LURES: Principle #7

You won't find many lures clearly associated with smallmouths the way rubber worms are with largemouths or, say, red-and-white Dardevles are with northern pike. But some artificials clearly work better than others.

The floating Rapala is widely used in shallow rivers and small ponds. It has the advantage of performing as either a surface lure or a shallow-running crankbait. Deep-diving crankbaits, which may run to 20 feet or more, account for a lot of smallmouths, too, and so do floating "silent" plugs, such as Zara Spooks.

Spinners may be the oldest of smallmouth lures. Today, "in-line" spinners, such as Mepps, Roostertails, and Panther Martins, continue to be top choices, although spinner baits are becoming increasingly popular—especially during the prespawn and early fall.

Jigs dressed with bucktail, hackle feathers, and marabou are effective because of the smallmouth's interest in crayfish. In southern reservoirs, where the influence of largemouth fishing seems most pronounced, jig and pigs (usually a heavy jig head with a pork rind trailer) are commonly used for fishing close to structures. Such "vertical fishing" also includes metal plugs such as the Silver Buddy and Little George.

These days, light tackle is standard for bait and spin fishers.

But the most popular jig arrangement—and arguably the most clearly identified "smallmouth lure"—involves a plastic trailer: a plastic grub, a Gitzit, a Tube, a Mister Twister, or something else next year. Anglers often use scent enhancements in concert with these jigs.

COLOR MATTERS: Principle #8

Smallmouths can be highly selective with regard to color. Many anglers, particularly trout fishers, grow up matching the color of the imitation to the color of the natural. That's often important in smallmouth fishing, too, but so is matching the color of the imitation to the color of the water.

In general, stained waters call for a brass or gold flash, and colors of black, brown, red, purple, pumpkinseed, orange, and yellow. Clear waters call for a chrome or silver flash and colors of white, pearl, blue, and smoke. Some of these colors, notably blue, black, yellow, and pumpkinseed, are "crossovers" (effective in both clear and stained waters). Silver works in stained waters if high-profile forage fish, such as juvenile shad or alewives, are present. Black is a good color on the surface at night and on the bottom any time. Yellow is a good general color, though for whatever reason, fluorescent chartreuse may be the most appealing of all.

In the clear water of the Great Lakes system, chartreuse is certainly the color of choice. Just as often, chartreuse is touted as an excellent choice for discolored water. And, while I've fished waters where other colors worked better, I've never fished a smallmouth water where chartreuse was a poor choice.

Perhaps the fluorescent glow suggests life in the darkened underwater world. My best guess is that fluorescent chartreuse contains other colors—blues, greens, pinks, pearl—that suggest prey to bass. Perhaps different water stains highlight one or more of these "effective" bass colors. This may well account for the effectiveness of other "unnatural colors," such as purple or hot orange. Who knows? Your guess is as good as mine.

In clear waters, it makes sense to imitate the forage first, stain second—although clear-water forage in general tends to be light colored with silver flashes, anyway. In stained waters, match the water first. An experience on the highly tannin waters of Vermont's Green River Reservoir exemplifies this point.

I sat in the bow of a canoe on an otherwise pleasant July afternoon while my friend Marcel Rocheleau sat in the stern and caught one bass after another on a fluorescent orange marabou streamer. Now this reservoir has perch, and the perch do have orange fins. But I think the success of this color had more to do with how the bright orange worked in concert with the tannin-stained water. Fluorescent orange would be my last choice for a wing color in clear-water lakes. And many of them have a strong forage base of perch with fins that are just as orange.

In short, color choice often has little to do with matching the natural forage, particularly in stained waters. This, of course, bothers the hell out of the trout fisherman in me, and for years I worried quite a bit about it. Meanwhile, pro bass fishers got rich nailing shiner-eating smallmouths on things like licorice-flavored plastic lizards, and I'm sure they slept just fine at night.

LIFELIKE TEXTURE AND ACTION
MATTER MORE: Principle #9

Tube jigs, as they're called, embody the most important elements of successful small-mouth bass fishing: Keep the lure, bait, or fly moving slowly; keep it near the bottom; and keep it appearing soft in texture with a lifelike movement.

That's important, and here's why. All gamefish—all predators, actually—feed on prey at the point it is most vulnerable. How they identify that vulnerability varies. For comparison, northern pike, which watch schools of baitfish, look for erratic *movement;* trout, which rise to insects, identify vulnerability through *shape,* as in the case of a spinner or an emerger with trailing husk; smallmouths feed on crayfish, preferring to take them at their point of vulnerability, i.e., when molting. As a result, they sense vulnerability through *texture*.

Hence the effectiveness of soft plastic lures, fur-bodied flies, and marabou streamers. In essence, soft texture works as a trigger, even when crayfish aren't the specific natural or even found in that particular water.

If texture is a trigger for bass thinking *crayfish,* lifelike action is a trigger for bass feeding on shiners. Mark Ridgway has spent time observing bass reactions to artificials, and he notes that they will follow a spinner for some distance, but will turn away if the movement drops off. The lifelike action of twister tails, Ridgway explains, often has a surprisingly strong effect; smallmouths attack in a rush as soon as the artificial comes into view.

BOATS AND CANOES: Principle #10

For some reason, there has always been this thing about boats and fly fishing not mixing. The fact is, nothing will improve your smallmouth fishing like a boat.

Some of the best smallmouth fishing in the country flows right through the heart of the eastern megalopolis. To get your own private stretch of water, get a boat or canoe or something that floats.

In Dick Sternberg's excellent book *Smallmouth Bass,* the first chapter (right after rods and reels) centers upon the kinds of boats, motors, and accessories useful for bass fishing. The last section of the chapter, one column of one page, discusses wading gear. Sternberg's emphasis reflects, if nothing else, the extent to which smallmouth fishing involves ponds, lakes, reservoirs, and navigable rivers.

This nice smallmouth took a streamer fly.

Fly fishing—in print, anyway—usually involves smallmouth rivers where the bass behave like trout. But lure and baitfishers know there's a whole other world of small-mouth fishing on the larger rivers, ponds, and lakes. The reason fly fishers have the smaller streams to themselves, frankly, is that spin fishers and bait casters don't want to bother with bass the size of brook trout.

I've never asked him, but I imagine that's also why Sternberg focused his first chapter on boats, motors, and accessories.

FLY FISHING?

Until recently, fly fishing for smallmouths has generally consisted of: 1) taking some of the least refined parts of fly fishing for trout and applying them to bassy-looking trout streams, or 2) taking the most refined parts of largemouth tactics and applying them to the shallows of ponds and lakes that we know have smallmouths.

In either case, the attitude is along the lines of "There. That ought to work." Well, in either case, it does—a little.

But fishing the wadeable rivers and the shorelines of lakes and ponds only scratches the surface of smallmouth fishing. There's simply a lot more to it than that.

5

The Right Stuff

RODS

As trout anglers moved to lighter fly rods during the 1950s and '60s, their bass fishing brethren continued to flail away with long, heavy slabs of fiberglass and bamboo. Largemouth fishing (which often did require substantial rods) set the tackle norms for all bass fishing. Anglers saw no other way, really, to cast the powder-puff hair moths and winged deer-hair flies that were standard fare for bass of either species.

In the 1950s, H. G. "Tap" Tapply made anglers aware of the virtues of a trimmed-down deer-hair fly. He also advocated the use of light tackle to cast this streamlined bug, opening up the sport to trout fishers, who found casting the largemouth rig of the day more like forking hay than fly fishing.

These days, modern graphite rods are not only powerful but comfortably light. A "smallmouth rod" has few specific requirements per se. It should be on the stiff side to facilitate setting the hook. And you do want to be able to handle weighted flies, streamers, and bugs in the size-2 to -6 range. If you do much fishing from a boat, a rod in the 8½- to 9½-foot range helps keep the line above your partners' heads and casts as well as can be hoped in the winds typical of open-water situations.

Like many anglers, I once went through a light-tackle phase, fishing for trout, smallmouths, and northerns with a 5-foot 3-inch glass Fenwick. Fortunately, I never hooked one of the latter, but I did catch quite a few smallmouth bass. And that light rod certainly put a new spin on a 1-pound bass.

These days I use a very substantial 9-foot 6-weight that takes a 7-weight floater and a 6-weight sink-tip. The rod throws the High-D sink-tip just fine; because it's such a club, it also handles the sink-tip with a lead core minihead attached. This one rod fishes smallmouth waters from streams to the Great Lakes.

In the end, you can spend about as much money on a smallmouth bass rod as you feel like spending. A 6- to 8-weight rod is fine, and for the most part so is a 5-weight and a 9-weight. When it comes to rod calibrations, smallmouths are very obliging fish. If anybody starts telling you otherwise, keep your wallet in your pocket.

LINES AND LEADERS

Lines, on the other hand, do matter, because they control the range of depths you can fish. Most smallmouth fishing involves a weight-forward floating line, a weight-forward sink-tip line, and a weight-forward full-sink line. Most of the time I can get by with just the first two.

I often end up fishing in water of 20–25 feet, sometimes as deep as 30 feet. Smallmouths in this depth are usually right on the bottom. Any of the modern express-rate full-sink lines will get you down there. So will a sink-tip if it has long head of 20 feet or more, characteristic of the Orvis Depth Charge and the Teeny Nymph line.

Miniheads, those 5- and 10-foot lead-core sections with loops, help a sink-tip handle water in the 20-plus range. Fly lines with loops at the end—you can either buy them that way or put on the loops yourself—make it easier to add or remove the lead-core sections.

A full-sink line can scrape the bottom of lakes and ponds. In areas of deep water with no current, this line is superior to a sink-tip, as you can keep your fly closer to the bottom longer. A full-sink also makes the best choice for drifting and trolling.

Great Lakes steelheaders use a 2-weight running line (so called because it forms the "running" part of a shooting taper) to deep-drift in heavy current. This line can also come in handy for smallmouth anglers facing similar conditions—i.e., drifting crayfish and hellgrammite imitations in deep water with heavy current. (See chapter 12 for a full description of rigging and using this line.)

As for leaders, a 3-foot length of 6-pound-test (3X) monofilament is really all you'll need for deep water and subsurface flies in general. The 6-pound-test tippet can withstand scrapes from the bottom, and the extra strength makes it easier to dislodge the fly from rocks.

You'll need a slightly longer leader when fishing on the surface or in situations in which presentation is important (when the bass are 20 feet down, presentation really

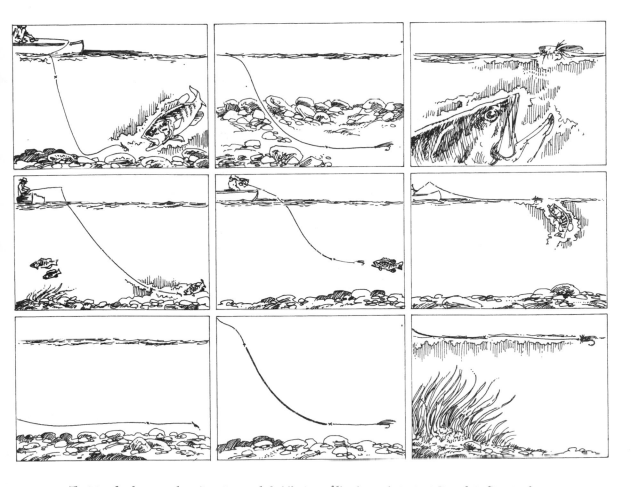

The type of rod you use doesn't matter much, but the type of line is very important. It needs to fit not only the situation, but also the fly and presentation: full-sink line, short leader with crayfish fly; sink-tip line, short leader with streamer; floating line, longer leader with bass bug on surface.

doesn't matter). A 7- to 9-footer generally does the trick with dry flies and bugs. The bushier your fly or bug, the more substantial the butt section you'll need.

Various situations require adjustments in tippet diameters. In general, a tippet need not be any finer than 3X for dries, although it should be a yard or so in length for flexibility in the drift.

For bugs and poppers, tippets are sized to handle the bug, not the bass. Eight- to 10-pound-test is usually about right. The loop system, with a braided 5-foot butt section and a 4-foot section of tippet, lets you build the various sections however you wish.

To some, the above leader specifications (as with earlier rod calibrations) may seem incomplete. And anglers may encounter clear-water conditions during late summer and fall that require a 4-pound-test tippet. But in general, smallmouths are not leader-shy. The real concern is that the tippet allow for an effective presentation. With bugs, that means permitting them to "turn over" at the end of a cast; with dries, that means permitting them to float drag-free on the surface; and with nymphs, that means permitting them to drift naturally in the current.

EXTRAS

Fly flotant, forceps, hook hone, clippers, penlight, bug dope, sunscreen, extra tippets, and other standard fly-fishing equipment comprise the rest of the angler's ensemble. Split shot in various sizes is indispensable. You really don't need a net. Bass can be landed easily with either a belly lift or a thumb and forefinger in the lower jaw.

If they're not wading, most smallmouth fly fishers find themselves in canoes. Silent, sleek, aesthetically correct, canoes are great for float-fishing, trolling streamers, and casting bugs and poppers.

Get them in some wind, however, and it becomes tough to do anything other than hold on to the gunnels. I don't know about you, but I find it difficult to fish subsurface flies (usually the best strategy in choppy water) while sitting in a canoe with my knees around my chin.

It makes sense to match craft with water, and you're definitely better off with more boat than you need. One of the first points to remember about open-water smallmouth fishing is that your boat takes you to (and from!) the fish. Many of the best smallmouth waters require at least a 13- to 16-foot boat; the biggest lakes and rivers can do with more boat than that.

Some of the best bass shoals on the bigger lakes and reservoirs face prevailing winds and 3-foot waves on even nice days. I've gotten along for years on the St. Lawrence River and Lake Ontario with a 13-foot boat, but I'm limited to areas close to shore. Most of my bass fishing friends have boats in the 15- to 22-foot range.

I love boats, always have, and so do most of the smallmouth fishers I know. You can relax, stretch out, fill the cooler, spend the day. On bigger lakes, reservoirs, and navigable rivers, the bigger the boat, the easier the fishing.

Boat fishing requires sneakers or boat shoes that won't slip on a wet surface. Double hauling from a rocking boat can definitely place you in a vulnerable position.

If you spend much time fishing from a boat, invest in (or make up) one of those saltwater stripping baskets. You can shoot line farther and you avoid constant tangles at your feet. There's no feeling more helpless than having fly line wrapped around your legs, the anchor line, and a half-filled can of beer while a 3-pound smallmouth does circus auditions off the bow.

FLIES

These days it's fashionable for fishing writers to worry about how we all carry too many flies. Fishing writers are probably right about this. But with dozens of boxes of flies crammed into my vest, I generally don't have a lot to say on this topic.

You don't need many flies to catch bass. But experimenting with various patterns is a lot of fun, and I usually pack along whatever I can comfortably lug.

Smallmouth anglers tend to stuff their boxes with bass bugs and then throw in a few streamers and wet flies in case the bugs don't work. On most days on most waters, reversing the emphasis will lead to more bass.

What follows comprises a basic selection of twenty-four patterns: three dry flies, seven bugs, seven streamers, and seven subsurface flies, including nymphs, wet flies, grubs, and crayfish patterns.

Some sixteen of the basic twenty-four patterns are included in the color plate section. The plates display flies designed for smallmouths and include forage-based patterns, such as the Marabou Matuka and Marabou Thunder Creek, generally not available commercially. Trout patterns that also work for smallmouths are not included in the plates but do appear in the basic fly section (e.g., White Wulff, Brown Hackle, Nine-three).

This basic assortment will meet most of the conditions and situations you'll find in smallmouth country. If you want to obsess beyond these two dozen, you're on your own.

Dry Flies

- Henryville Special—#10, 14
- White Wulff—#8, 10, 12
- Irresistible—#8

This list starts growing quickly if you fish smallmouth streams very often.

A selection of smallmouth dry flies: from left to right, Henryville Special, White Wulff, Irresistible.

Bass Bugs

- Tapply Hair Bug (natural deer hair; white and yellow)—#1, 4
- Most Whit Hair Bug—#1
- Cork Popper (white, black)—#1 or 2
- Sneaky Pete (yellow)—#1 or 2
- Dahlberg Diver—#2, 3X long
- Orvis Swimming Frog—#1
- Messinger Bucktail Frog—#1

The Tapply Hair Bug is the basic bass bug tied with clipped gray or brown hair from the white-tailed deer. It meets a range of topwater situations. Dave Whitlock's Most Whithair series is an elaboration on this theme. The Most Whithair series comes in all shapes, sizes, and colors. Chartreuse, yellow, brown, and purple are my favorites.

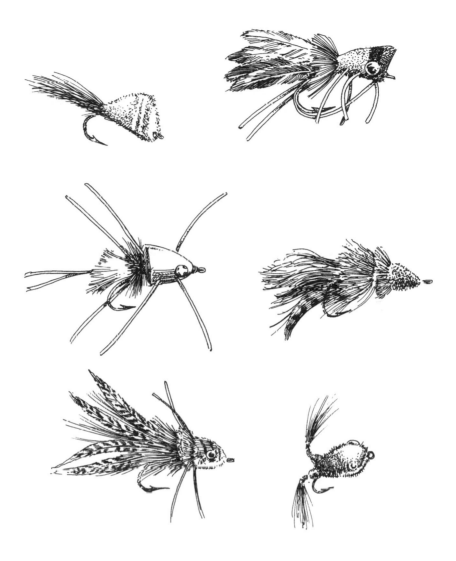

A selection of smallmouth bugs: from left to right, top to bottom, Tapply Hair Bug, Most Whit Hair Bug, Sneaky Pete, Dahlberg Diver, Orvis Swimming Frog, Messinger Frog.

Magazine articles often emphasize the need for cork poppers at certain times, though I must admit to liking everything about hair over cork—the sound it makes when it hits the water, the way it floats, the *gerblub*! it makes when twitched. True, a cork body never gets soggy—which may be helpful if the fish are coming fast. We should have more such problems.

To my way of thinking, cork makes a better slider or Sneaky Pete, a modern-day rendition of the seventy-five-year-old Wilder-Dilg cork minnow. The Dahlberg Diver is a terrific hair-bodied modification of this bug and may well be the most versatile small-mouth floater we have.

Frog imitations have long entranced fly fishers and fishers in general. They play to our fantasies, and it could be that frogs have made more magazine cover appearances over the years than all other smallmouth and largemouth foods put together. Joe Messinger's two-toned hair frog (gray on top, white or yellow on the bottom) was one of the earliest and most successful of the frog imitations, and it still works today.

Streamers

- Nine-three—#4, 4X long
- Marabou streamer (yellow and gold, white and silver, gray and silver, chartreuse and silver, orange and silver)—#2, 6X long; #4, 4X long
- Muddler Minnow—#4, 3X long
- Marabou Muddler (yellow and gold, black and gold, olive brown and gold)—#4, 4X long
- Clouser Minnow (Ultra, chartreuse and white, Foxee)—#4, 4X long
- Woolly-headed Sculpin—#4, 4X long

Feathered streamers all catch bass. I just happen to like the Nine-three; many anglers prefer a Gray Ghost.

The Marabou streamer—white wing/silver body—may be the closest thing to a generic smallmouth streamer. Marabou moves even when the fly doesn't. The material seems alive, suggests life itself.

The Muddler Minnow imitates everything from sculpins to dragonfly nymphs to crayfish. It's an important pattern, particularly in rivers.

The combination of the Muddler form and marabou wing—the Marabou Muddler—marked a clear departure from the eastern smelt and dace forms, which until the 1970s dominated streamer dressings (for trout, salmon, and, de facto, bass). It can be fished along the bottom as a darter/madtom/sculpin imitation or on the surface in the evenings when smallmouths might be inclined toward the top.

In some rivers, sculpins and darters are very important forage. The Woolly-headed Sculpin is the latest imitation and quite successful in moving flows.

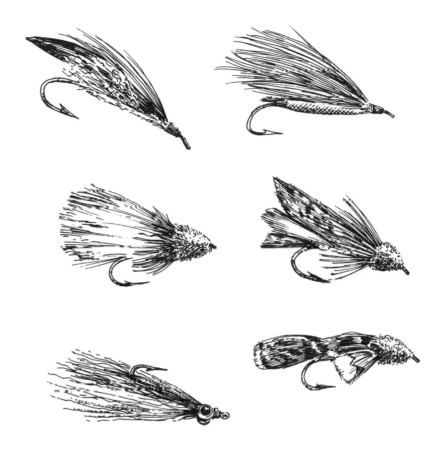

A selection of streamers: from left to right, top to bottom, Nine-three, Marabou Streamer, Marabou Muddler, Muddler Minnow, Clouser Minnow, Woolly-headed Sculpin.

The Clouser Minnow makes an excellent all-around baitfish imitation. A weighted head gets it down there, and the big eyes and glittery, transparent body/wing give it a good look. Attached at the head, the hair works well with the weighted head, not unlike a jig—though no fly fishers would call it that, would they?

Wets

- Bead-head Woolly Bugger (olive, chartreuse, brown, black)—#4 and 8, 3X long
- Sparrow—#6, 2X long
- Brown Hackle—#10

A selection of sinking flies: from left to right, top to bottom, Bead-head Woolly Bugger, Brown Hackle, Sparrow, Clouser Swimming Nymph, Brooks Stonefly Nymph, Hellgrammite, Crayfish, Sparkle Grub.

- Clouser Swimming Nymph (brown)—#10, 2X long
- Brooks' Stonefly Nymph (black)—#4, 3X long
- Hellgrammite—#4, 4X long
- Crayfish—#4, 3X long
- Sparkle Grub—#2, 3X long

The Woolly Bugger with a bead head and some flash in the tail is one of the best patterns for river smallmouths. It suggests a variety of forage, depending on color. In black, it imitates hellgrammites and leeches; in olive/brown, sculpins/darters and crayfish; in white/chartreuse with Flashabou, shiners. Lifelike movement in hackles, legs, and tails often triggers a strike.

Traditionally, the smallmouth's vulnerability to such quivering and undulation has been attributed to defects in character. After all, American dry-fly fishing began with the stiffest hackles and burnished quill bodies and flies that were fished upstream only. Remnants of this canon survive today, caddis fished downstream notwithstanding. Whereas trout scrutinize every offering, bass, poor unfortunates, are given to impulse.

As noted in chapter 3, the smallmouth's attraction to "soft" materials has nothing to do with character defects and everything to do with a smallmouth's own idea of selectivity. Soft texture is an important trigger for smallmouths—probably more than it is for trout—and in general fur, partridge hackle, and marabou make the best nymph and wet-fly patterns.

Jack Gartside's Sparrow is an excellent example of a "soft-textured" smallmouth fly. So is the Brown Hackle (tied with brown grouse hackle). The Clouser Swimming Nymph, basically a nymph's body with an ostrich plume tail, has terrific action.

You should carry some stonefly nymph and hellgrammite patterns if you fish streams and rivers much. The Brooks' Stonefly makes a good choice for the former (I often tie it in brown and black), the Murray's Hellgrammite for the latter. The hellgrammite pattern described in the Fly Pattern Appendix offers a more imitative outline and works well on a dead drift.

You'll definitely want some crayfish patterns for midsummer, particularly if you fish in lakes or big rivers. The Clouser Crayfish is a good pattern, as are any number available commercially. The pattern described in chapter 10 and appendix C worked well for me.

The Sparkle Grub is my own design and a useful fly for lakes and big rivers. (See chapter 12 for a full discussion.) Other grub-type imitations fill this deep-water "worm/leech" niche, too. Holschlag's Hackle Jig is a good choice, as is Whitlock's Hare Pup, which makes a good leech imitation.

*　*　*

So that's what I think. You could easily add or subtract patterns from the list and make a good case for the move.

A lot of fly fishers find a list of smallmouth flies bordering on the ridiculous. Pearls before swine. My trout and salmon fishing friends from northern New England are always saying things like, "You should see the fly I use for bass."

For people *into* smallmouth fishing, it's hard to ignore the power of fly patterns. It's like that, of course, with any type of fly fishing.

Common sense says that it's the person presenting the fly that makes the difference. But another little voice keeps saying, "Come on. Come on. Put on the fly. You know which one. What are you waiting for? Put it on, for Christ's sake."

As with most seductions, common sense doesn't stand much of a chance.

The mantra of "best fly" started for me with my first fly-caught fish. It came from a small creek that twisted through the back pasture of my Uncle George's dairy farm in upstate New York, several miles from the St. Lawrence River. Creek chubs and dace were the quarry.

Early one summer I went there with some old brook trout flies I'd found somewhere—a Parmachene Belle, a Scarlet Ibis, and a McGinty. On a trout fishing trip that spring, my dad had explained that there was no way any smart old brown trout was going to strike flies designed to attract turn-of-the-century brook trout. "All you're going to catch on those flies is chubs," he said.

Down at the farm that summer I did just that—on purpose. I used an old spinning rod and a length of monofilament. It was just like fly fishing. (It *was* fly fishing!) I'd let the fly float along and twitch it over the deep spot next to the clay bank. Dace and chubs, some of which were all of 5 inches long, would bounce up and nail those flies in quicksilver turns.

The difference in the effectiveness of the three flies was undeniable. The McGinty was worthless; it wouldn't even get a nudge from the dace. The bright red Ibis might get a dace now and then. But the Parmachene Belle, with its yellow body and red-and-white wing, outfished the other two by a wide margin. Somewhere in every fly fisher's past is such a moment—dangerous, delicious, when he or she sees in instantaneous clarity that one fly works better than others.

I always saved that Parmachene Belle (once it got gummed up, it was impossible to float) for the deeper holes down the creek, where there was some grass and bigger creek chubs. And when I left that Parmachene Belle buried in a log, I quit fishing chubs.

So. Before catching my first trout, bass, or even sunfish on a fly, I was already accustomed to seeing *pattern* as the key ingredient in fly-fishing success. *American Angler* editor Art Scheck has it right. "People love to read about flies," he says. "It never occurs to them that they need to learn to present flies better, improve their casting, or further develop their array of good knots. They'll kill for a new fly pattern."

Perhaps it reflects the well-educated, information-saturated angler of today; or perhaps the modern angler's sublime confidence in his or her abilities. Whatever the case, most of us can't wait to get to the good part about which patterns work best. At least that's how I feel when I read articles.

Casting, knots. It's all so mechanical. Where's the artistry? Presentation is told to us, taught to us, and descriptions of how to do it sound condescending or patronizing. They put me to sleep.

But flies are different. There are thousands to choose from; if you tie your own, tens of thousands. In the end it's a matter we ourselves design.

Or, more accurately perhaps, a matter of how we design ourselves.

6

Spring and Early-Summer Fishing

PRESPAWN

I n the natural rhythm of things, summer was traditionally the season for bass fishing. A peek at the fishing regulations in 1921, for instance, shows the season remaining closed until July as far south as Virginia.

But spring fishing is becoming more popular these days, in part because it offers a good chance at some big bass. I prefer to fish smallmouths during the summer, to tell the truth, and it's only since 1980, when I moved to Massachusetts, that I've done any spring smallmouth fishing to speak of.

Last spring I spent several days fishing the prespawn on the Quabbin, a sprawling, clear-water reservoir in central Massachusetts, with my friends Ray Coppinger and Stan Warner.

The first day started off warm and sunny, with the forecast calling for an afternoon front. Perfect.

We debated where to start. Quabbin smallmouths share habitat with landlocked salmon during the spring, so this is not exactly the kind of decision you want to rush into. The discussion was lively. We all teach at the same college, and by the end of the year arguing comes naturally. Open your mouth and out pops a counterpoint.

With the semester over, fates decided, and graduation a week away, obsessing about something without consequences felt as good as spending someone else's money.

This prespawn smallmouth took a marabou streamer in 15 feet of water.

The first stop, we agreed (finally), should be an area of gravel flats on the Quabbin's north end. Stan had been fishing the area several times the previous week, doing well with plastic shad fished on light spinning tackle.

We began drifting over the drop-offs at the edge of the flats, fishing the edges in 10–15 feet. Ray and Stan each nailed a bass; I stood in the bow and worked a streamer ahead of the boat.

The surface was glassy. Clear. So calm you could feel the boat rock when someone followed through on a cast. Curls of mist lifted from the eastern side of the reservoir. The granite hillsides glowed with frog-green leaves. Earlier we had seen a coyote on a sidehill, heard the thundering gobble of a spring turkey; it was hard not to be rubber-necking around for wildlife.

Bang! My rod gyrates in my hands and I have this 3-pound smallmouth sloshing across the surface. I let the line slip through my fingers, get the fish on the reel, and work it to the boat. After one last halfhearted jump, the bass is done and I am holding, then releasing, my first smallmouth of the season.

Like this fish, most prespawn smallmouths simply do not fight with the vigor of bass caught a month later because of the cold water. Interestingly, the fish still jump when hooked; they just don't jump as high or as cleanly as summer-caught bass. They would not get good marks from the eastern European judges.

My friend Mark Feinstein, a professor of animal behavior, calls jumping an involuntary motor reflex or spasm that fish experience in response to the hook. In cold water the response is the same, the behavior executing it simply more sluggish.

The fish has no choice about this jumping business, in other words. I hope this doesn't disappoint those who like to think that fish jump in a strategic and grandiloquent effort to throw the hook. Sorry guys.

WARMING WATERS

At no other time of year do so many good-sized fish gather along predictable structures. The biggest are females, ripe with eggs. Smaller males also move in, and they are hungry, too.

Smallmouths may occasionally take crayfish (particularly in southern lakes and reservoirs), but the abundant-and-available rule means that, in general, prespawn fish feed on baitfish or small panfish.

Marabou streamers in sizes 2–4, 6X long, make good starting choices. With no young-of-the-year baitfish or panfish around, any prey fish is bound to be good sized. Start with a fast-sink line (or sink-tip) and unweighted streamer flies; the presentation usually needs to be deep and slow, and with no extra weight on the flies you can really slow things down if necessary. Regular 3-inch strips, with a brief pause every 3 or 4 feet and a longer ten-second pause every 20 feet, is a good starting retrieve. Slow *and* erratic, in other words.

If you're fishing from a drifting boat or canoe, avoid the temptation to hang the streamer over the side and let the wind do your fishing. You'll catch some bass on a steady-drifting, high-riding streamer fished this way, but you'll catch a lot more on bottom-oriented, erratic retrieves. The trick is to fish ahead of the drifting boat. (For a full

Smallmouths staging off the lip of a spawning area can be taken on streamers fished slow and deep. Often this leads to some of the biggest bass of the year.

discussion of this method, see chapter 12.) Hits, by the way, often come as soon as you begin the retrieve.

But we're getting ahead of ourselves. You've got to find the fish first. The northern ends of lakes often warm first, as the warm southern wind blows the warmer waters north. Think *spawning habitat,* not *feeding shoal.* Look for gravel, rubble, and clamshell bays in ponds and lakes; in rivers and streams look for gravel bars and pockets protected from the flow. As noted in chapter 3, spawning depth generally ranges from 4–12 feet. My own inclination is to start with the biggest possible spawning area in any given water or section of water.

Once you've identified a spawning area, work in concentric circles until you locate possible staging areas. In rivers, that means the edges of deep pools, outside the main flow. In shallow lakes and ponds, it can mean obstructions, like brushpiles or boat docks. In deeper lakes and reservoirs, a 10- to 30-foot drop-off on the lip of a spawning bay often serves as a primary staging area for prespawn fish; this was where we found smallmouths at the Quabbin. The bass will hold right on the drop-off. The warmer the day, the closer the water temperature to 60 degrees, the farther up on the drop-off the fish will be.

Prespawn fish are on a temperature-driven time clock. As the surface reaches the mid-50s, smallmouths become increasingly active in the staging areas. Once the temperature climbs into the upper 50s, the spawning urge dominates their behavior. Feeding seems less of a priority, and fishing can suffer as a result.

That's just what happened to us that morning on the Quabbin. We began to see bass up on the sides of the spawning shoals, and they displayed little interest in our flies and lures. I slipped a thermometer into the water; it read 58 degrees. Stan tried live bait, and when a smallmouth ignored the shiner wriggling in its face, we knew it was time to revise our plan.

"Let's try the backside of that island," Stan said, nodding to an acre-sized chunk of hardscrabble that bordered the shoal. "The water might be a few degrees cooler. And I know they spawn in those little bays near shore." We motored over and found 55-degree temperatures.

We drifted the shoreline, trying to stay over the drop-off right where you'd lose sight of the bottom. The depth was between 10 and 15 feet, and the bass were there. We caught a pair on the first drift.

The fishing picked up as the day clouded over and the front approached. Marabou streamers and plastic shads both accounted for some good smallmouths. Stan lost a bass right at the boat that probably topped 6 pounds.

Later we debated the cause of the on-again/off-again bass that day. Finding cooler water temperatures certainly seemed to help matters. We didn't see any bass actually up on the spawning area at the second spot, suggesting that lower water temperatures was the key. The approaching front appeared to spark a general increase in activity, too. Perhaps we timed it just right.

In any case, prespawn fishing is inherently transitional. Prespawn smallmouth anglers need spring to keep progressing (a cold snap simply shuts down the fishing), but often find themselves trying to slow down the progression. We managed to take advantage of the fact that spring water temperatures can vary in different areas of a big body of water. We were able to stretch things out just right.

BASS ON THE BEDS

On the Quabbin, as elsewhere, the consistency of prespawn fishing tends to diminish as smallmouths actually begin spawning. This is particularly true for the larger females.

Not all the bass in a lake are on the exact same reproductive schedule, however. At any given time bass in some areas may be just preparing to spawn, while in others males may be already guarding the nests. You can usually find some fishing by covering different spawning areas.

This canoe fisherman used a hair bug to land this spawning-time smallmouth.

As for techniques in shallow water, marabou streamers on sink-tips fished near boulders produce bass. Black Woolly Buggers or leech patterns also work. And poppers can be excellent choices immediately following actual spawning.

Accurate casting, generally not an issue in smallmouth fishing, is important when fishing for males guarding the nests. Some anglers believe that streamers, Woolly Buggers, and leech patterns draw males off the nests because the naturals they imitate represent such threats to the eggs and fry. Maybe. But they won't draw them from very far.

If you locate nests in shallow water—5 feet and under, say—popper fishing can be exceptional. Actually, you can take fish on poppers in deeper water, too, depending on conditions (calm water, as you'd expect, is better than a ruffled surface) and the behavior of the bass. Smallmouths in some lakes are simply more inclined to feed from the surface.

For a male guarding the nest, a popping bug can represent an unsavory character intent on eating its charges. There is little pattern to preferences. On some days, certain colors do indeed work better, although it's tough to go wrong with yellow or white or, in hair, with natural gray.

This nest-guarding behavior has, over the years, reinforced our notion of the bass as fun to catch, but hardly a challenge of the same order as trout or salmon. In years past, a fly fisher's only encounter with smallmouths often occurred during nest-guarding—the one time of the season that bass were in reach of floating lines and poppers, which was pretty much the extent of smallmouth fishing equipment for many years. Now, fly fishers appear increasingly interested in fishing for smallmouths during the summer, when spawning is over and, I suppose, trout fishing slows down.

POSTSPAWN

The northwest wind kicked up a chop on the top end of the Quabbin. It was cold for June.

"Right in here," said Ray Coppinger, eyeing the gravel bay. "Right near this rocky point with that pyramid boulder."

It was the spot where, two weeks earlier, we'd hit all those smallmouths. Now that the spawn was over, we hoped to be back in business, though we were braced for the worst. And we got it. Two hours without a strike.

We anchored and cast some more. I finally caught an 8-incher on a Woolly Bugger. "Let's work down this next shore," Ray said.

We did, but the fishing showed no improvement. The only fish we saw were small males. They were in 10 feet of water and, more to the point, weren't taking. Anything.

A black Woolly Bugger accounted for this postspawn smallmouth.

The wind stayed steady out of the northwest, making for one of those bright, pretty, good-to-be-alive days that absolutely suck for fishing. We were back at the dock by noon.

Uh, postspawn bass can be a challenge.

In larger, deeper reservoirs like the Quabbin, postspawn smallmouths scatter along gradual drop-offs, where they recuperate from the rigors of the preceding two months. They show neither the appetite of the prespawn period nor the defined schooling of summer. Throw in a cold front like Ray and I faced on the Quabbin, and you're better off staying home.

If the urge to fish strikes and you find yourself in a boat before you can collect your faculties, look for postspawn smallmouths in areas of boulder, gravel, and rubble marked by gradual changes in depth from, say, 10 to 15 feet. Sparse weed beds can be a key indicator. Offshore gravel shoals, always good spots, are well worth trying. Finally, postspawn smallmouths also gather in the lower stretches of tributaries.

Baitfish are the most common forage in lakes and rivers, so streamer flies make a good choice. As during the prespawn, go big; size 4, 6X is about right, at least in the bigger lakes, reservoirs, and rivers.

Late June is a great time to be on a smallmouth river.

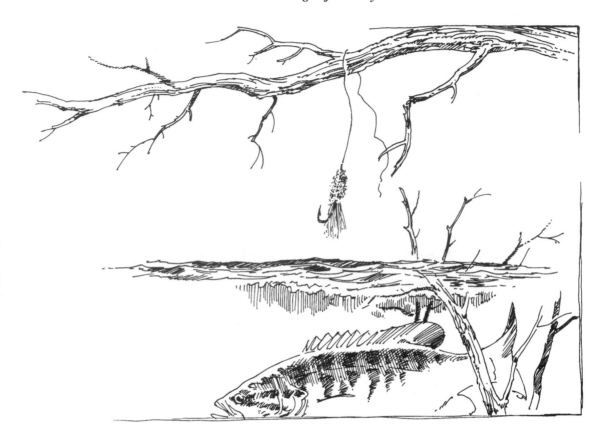

Bug-fishing memories.

Think *marabou*. Since it can be fished very slowly and still produce action, marabou is the best choice for working a gravel patch in a weed bed—a top postspawn location—where the fly only has a few yards to do its thing. A marabou streamer fished very slowly or a Sparkle Grub (see chapter 12) retrieved in tiny hops are both good choices.

Other times, it makes sense to cover territory. Shoreline drifting with the wind will help you find scattered smallmouths better than most any strategy. Casting beyond the sweet spots and letting the wind-driven boat pull your streamer into action can be an effective technique. The Gray Ghost, Nine-three, and other featherwing streamers often do quite well in this situation.

As for retrieves, a steady procession of 2- to 3-inch strips is a standard. If that doesn't work, try a foot-long strip and a longer drop—particularly if you're fishing next to structures like boulders, docks, and so forth.

Actually, I've always thought streams, rivers, and shallow flows offer the best postspawn fishing of all, if for no other reason than that locating smallmouths is easier in smaller waters and flows. Rivers have a richness about them in June, and the smallmouths seem to respond to the profusion of aquatic insects.

Rivers, flows, ponds, and lakes with extensive areas of shallow water often have good surface fishing during the postspawn. Last June I got a chance to spend a couple hours after dinner casting bugs on an Adirondack flowage. I shoved off in a canoe, fleeing the black flies. Out on the flow, the wind had died. It was a warm evening, buggy and fishy.

I worked out some line, casting toward shore. When I laid the bug next to a fallen tree, the boil of a good fish showed at the surface. The bug rocked on the disturbance.

A twitch, a pop, another boil, and this time there was strength on the line, and a fine smallmouth, dark as a spruce root, sprang into the air. The bass got tangled in some brush almost immediately, and I was forced to break it off.

But the moment had been perfect.

Still is, as a matter of fact.

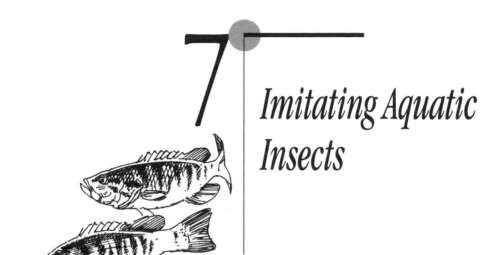

Imitating Aquatic Insects

I suppose the first question is "Why bother?"

Nearly all studies find aquatic insects playing an essential role in the diet of juvenile bass and a peripheral (at best) role in the diet of adult smallmouths. A smallmouth doesn't reach the 20-inch mark by pounding down caddis larvae.

One thought: This assessment of the relative importance of insects and baitfish/crayfish often rests upon data expressed in volume, not numbers of food items. The gap closes a bit when the latter serves as the frame of reference. Some studies do show insects as important during spring— a time when they are most available, and crayfish, not coincidentally, are not. Shallow, fertile rivers increase the likelihood of smallmouths feeding on insects.

As for how to do it, anglers are indebted to Harry Murray's *Fly Fishing for Smallmouth Bass*. Murray's book offers a comprehensive system for imitating the aquatic insects (and other forage) important to smallmouths.

As for the experience of fishing smallmouths in streams, you may find the issue less one of matching the hatch than one of approximating the forage type and behavior. So there is complexity, though you won't see many smallmouth fishers wading around with furrowed brows. The emphasis falls more on fishing than on fly selection.

You don't need the gear and flies required for trout fishing, no rattling into battle with every fly pattern and gizmo known to man stuffed into your vest. During the summer, you can leave your waders home and fish wet with just your felt-soled wading shoes. If the river is big enough, by all means float a canoe.

Wading wet is often the most sensible approach for midsummer smallmouth rivers.

DRY FLIES

Several hatches of mayflies and caddis may be locally important. To the south, in the traditional smallmouth rivers of the mid-Atlantic states and the upper South, the damselfly joins the list of important insects. In fact, Harry Murray calls the damselfly the most important surface natural for river smallmouths.

The white fly, or white millers (*Ephoron leukon*), may be the most important mayfly. A warm-water insect, it appears in late July and early August in rivers across smallmouth range. In southern New York, Pennsylvania, and Virginia, the hatches can be like blizzards. A size-12 White Wulff is a suitable and durable imitation.

This can be a maddening hatch. Once, on the lower Lamoille River in Vermont, I stepped into the water to find literally thousands of duns about and not a single fish rising for them.

White Millers* (Ephoron leukon) *bring good numbers of smallmouths to the surface during late summer on the rivers in the Mid-Atlantic states.

I figured the bass were feeding beneath the surface, so that night I tied white emergers and nymphs into the wee hours. The next evening I was right back at it—flies everywhere, fish nowhere again. Flogging the water with nymphs and emergers resulted in a 10-inch fallfish at dusk, and a black marabou took a single smallmouth right at dark. In this instance, the smallmouths simply ignored the hatch.

Not so on other rivers to the south. On the Susquehanna River in Pennsylvania, for example, this hatch brings some excellent fishing, usually around the first week in August. As Charles Meck, sage of Pennsylvania hatches, has noted, the white fly is an active insect, with the emerger shooting to the surface and the dun dancing just above the water.

This behavior actually helps anglers address the problem of the imitation getting lost among so many naturals on the water. Twitching or skittering the fly about often gets some attention from bass inundated with duns. (Even when nothing is hatching, you can sometimes "pound up" bass by skating high-floating flies across the surface.)

Standard dry flies work in most match-the-hatch situations—smallmouths are not particularly selective in this respect—and the Irresistible, Adams, and Wulffs usually do the trick. The Henryville Special will handle most caddis hatches, and Whitlock's

Damsel Fly offers an excellent imitation of the natural damsel. You may want to carry some ant imitations if you fish the Susquehanna and other mid-Atlantic rivers in September.

A small popper, deer-hair bug, or even streamer will often take rising smallmouths—a tribute to the fish's opportunism. A floating Muddler Minnow is a good general pattern; it takes fish on a dead drift as well as when twitched along. A nymph swimming beneath the surface will take them, too, sometimes when nothing else will.

I encountered this situation years ago on a Vermont pond named Lake Eden, which held both smallmouth bass and trout. On warm, still evenings in July, rises would appear at a shallow gravel bar in the middle of the pond.

I watched the action from shore one night and brought my canoe along the next. Out on the shoal, the fish had started to pop. The only flies on the surface were black caddis, close to size 18, so it seemed reasonable to assume that the fish were trout.

A small Adams on 5X took a pasty-looking freshly stocked rainbow, barely 9 inches long. I caught its twin, then another. As usual, the swirls of the fish I wasn't catching looked bigger.

I cut back the leader to 3X, tied on a tan, soft-hackled Woolly Worm—a fly that happened to be on my vest, it being *Potamanthus* time on the nearby Lamoille. On my first cast, the line twitched and a swirl appeared near the fly.

"Those little stocked fish," I thought. "Christ, they'll take anything."

But this one had some weight, and suddenly a nice smallmouth vaulted out of the water.

I landed several more smallmouths that evening. To this day I have no idea if they really were taking the caddis. In years to come, I'd have similar experiences at a number of the area ponds, usually catching a few bass, but seldom in proportion to the overall surface activity.

I experimented with a number of flies, too. Matching the small caddis resulted in nothing but stocked rainbows. The smallmouths would come to bass bugs and to Muddler Minnows on still nights, but the soft-hackled Woolly Worms retrieved just beneath the surface usually worked best.

SWIMMERS AND DRIFTERS

If soft-hackled flies catch smallmouths in lakes and ponds, they work even better in rivers. The gentle riffles that wash along the sides of boulders and curl into eddies clearly call for soft-textured flies. Pattern seems less important than the overall impression of life.

A soft-backled swimmer accounted for this smallmouth.

The first swimmer/drifter I ever used for river smallmouths was the Sparrow, a soft as an-old-slipper creation of fly-tying wizard Jack Gartside.

I met the Sparrow on the lower Lamoille River in Vermont, thanks to fishing companion Pete Laszlo (not long after Laszlo had written an article in *The Roundtable* describing this fly). Laszlo used it to nail three nice smallmouths beneath the base of a falls at the head of a big pool.

In retrospect, his success makes sense. What a perfect place to dead-drift a generic soft hackle. It calls to mind the caddis-eating smallmouths lying beneath the falls (see chapter 3). Unlike smallmouths elsewhere in the river, they fed extensively on caddis because of the volume of insects trying to hatch upstream that were swept down in the current. It's quite likely that the fish beneath the falls on the Lamoille had the same idea.

Any fur nymph would probably work in this sort of situation. Gold-ribbed Hare's Ear, Leisenring Spider, and caddis pupa patterns are all good choices; if there is any principle in fly selection, it involves capitalizing on smallmouths' predilection for sensing the vulnerability of prey through texture. As noted earlier, the breathing-with-the-current quality of fur, marabou, partridge hackle, and other materials can provide a powerful trigger in this regard.

Bob Clouser's Swimming Nymph is a "soft-fly" with a lot of movement; so are the patterns in Harry Murray's Strymph series. These flies have ostrich herl rear ends and, as Murray notes, the fibers cling together, unlike marabou, and let you swim the nymph *with* the current—a highly effective retrieve, by the way.

To do this, face the flow, work out some line—not too much—and cast upstream. Try to put the fly above the spot where you think the bass might be. The trick is to get the fly drifting in the current without drag, then make it swim with the flow. I do my best

Fly-fishing author Tom Fuller with a Connecticut River smallmouth taken on a soft-hackled wet fly.

to keep the rod high and experiment with retrieves. The most effective one is often just a hair faster than the flow—at least that's been my experience.

You can also fish upstream and across and, in effect, pull the fly into the current, swimming it back to you with the flow. Or you can fish directly across the current. To do this, work out some line and make a cast quartering upstream. Mend the line so that the fly sinks a bit and drifts down naturally. When the fly is almost directly across the stream from you, strip it back across the current. Try to retrieve the fly so that it swims more than is pushed by the current—though you might find it useful to pause between strips. Strikes can come at any point, but often as not they occur just after the first strip or two.

Like everybody else, I fish across and down more than I should. Fortunately, on many streams and on most days, a Bead-head Woolly Bugger can turn this into a pretty good smallmouth strategy.

Given the significance of stonefly nymphs, hellgrammites, crayfish, and sculpins, the Woolly Bugger in black, brown, and olive might be the best all-around fly available to the wading smallmouth angler. I've had good luck in the last two years, in particular, with a soft-hackled, mottled-brown Woolly Bugger. I usually add some brown Flashabou and a gold bead head, too.

As I said, I fish it across and down quite a bit, but the Woolly Bugger works quite well upstream and across stream, too. Doubtless I get more upstream strikes than I realize. Sometimes I pick them out as simple hesitations in the line. Predictably, a lot of strikes come right on the swing. You may feel slight nips on the marabou tail. Don't dismiss them as chubs. Try to hold steady on the nips for a moment, then drop the fly back a few inches, then steady up. What you think is a fallfish could well turn out to be a nice bass.

Smallmouths seldom take a fly with an arms-out-of-your-sockets hit, anyway, unless you and the fish happen to be going in different directions. Once I was working a subsurface imitation in New York's Salmon River, a water known primarily for its steelhead fishing. When my drifting line slowed slightly, I assumed it had caught on a small mat of moss floating in front of me. When I shook my rod to free the line I found myself attached to a 20-inch bass—still the biggest smallmouth I've taken with my feet in waders.

I thought I'd hooked a weed.

BOUNCING BOTTOM

While collecting some hellgrammites to photograph this past October, I had a chance to get a closer look at the bottom of a bass stream—and it was most enlightening. I went to one of my favorite stretches of broken water in a river near my home, put down a nymph screen, and began kicking rocks. No hellgrammites drifted into the mesh, but plenty of stonefly nymphs did—a half dozen or more on every try.

After an hour of trying, I finally found a pair of hellgrammites beneath a big rock in heavy water. (You can see one of them on page 86.) But on the way home that night, my thoughts turned to the stonefly nymphs. There sure were a lot of them.

On this river and others, larger stonefly nymphs in the genera *Pteronarcys* and *Perla* can be well worth imitating. The naturals are a mouthful—they can live for three years before hatching—and that makes them the one "trout" nymph that can consistently draw attention from adult bass. Tom Fuller speculates in his new book, *Under-*

Stonefly nymphs (and other subsurface flies) are at their best when drifted drag-free through a boulder-strewn stretch using an upstream presentation.

water Flies, that molting stonefly nymphs (they appear cream colored, almost albino-like) are particularly appealing to trout. And Tom has always insisted that smallmouths like them even better than trout do. It is certainly worth considering, given the small-mouth's predilection for soft texture.

Stonefly nymphs require oxygenated runs and tolerate water as warm as 78 degrees. Of their habitats, boulder-framed slicks and pocket water make the best fishing. Bouncing an imitation along the bottom of these stretches can produce fish during mid-day, when the river is otherwise pretty quiet.

Most fishers agree that the best way to do this is with a floating line, a 6- to 9-foot leader, and split shot pinched on a short dropper off the tippet. It's important to cast well upstream from the target so that the fly is tumbling along the bottom when it reaches the shadows of the boulders. Although I find strike indicators vaguely irritating, they do increase hookups on such presentations.

It's been my experience that deep, strong currents reduce the effectiveness of indicators, because the weight needed to get the fly down often takes the indicator with it. I generally compromise by using a fluorescent orange tube at the end of my line and trying to keep it in the surface tension. Some anglers report good luck using a pinch of commercial floating starch paste; it can be smeared on leader knots.

THE STRANGE CASE OF THE HELLGRAMMITE

Without doubt the hellgrammite is the most significant smallmouth nymph, at least in terms of things anglers can productively imitate.

Murray's Hellgrammite is a standard selection, as is Dave Whitlock's pattern. Bob Clouser's hellgrammite imitation has proven successful; so has Farrow Allen's. And these are just a few of them. Like many smallmouth fishers, I came up with my own hellgrammite, and it works, too.

The hellgrammite, actually the larval form of the dobsonfly (*Corydalus cornutus*), often grows to a length of 3 inches. It is a fierce-looking little critter with a rubbery body, a shell-like wing case and head covering, and distinct mandibles. Coloration varies from jet black to dark moss to deep chocolate brown.

The dobsonfly's range extends from the eastern seaboard to the Rocky Mountains, from Canada south to Mexico. Oxygenated stream riffles, with combinations of gravel and flat rock, make the best habitat. Hellgrammites feed opportunistically on various aquatic insects, often chironomid (midge larvae). They do their best to avoid leaving the cover of rocks.

Hellgrammites make excellent bait and serve as the basis for very effective fly patterns.

Like other aquatic nymphs, hellgrammites are largest and most active just before pupation, i.e., in late spring and early summer. They leave the stream and pupate under the soil, beneath rocks, or in hollow logs. The adults hatch within two weeks, usually at night. After mating, females lay eggs on overhanging trees, and the larvae eventually drop into the stream. In northern areas, hellgrammites have two- or three-year life cycles; in warmer southern waters, only one- or two-year.

It's no secret that adult bass really go for hellgrammites. They have a reputation as the best of all baits for river bass, and seining and selling them is an important local industry on some rivers. It almost goes without saying that the hellgrammite is an important forage for river smallmouths. That, in fact, is the popular explanation for its success as a live bait. But research suggests something else.

A 1993 study on the New River in West Virginia—an outstanding smallmouth river, by the way—found smallmouths consuming less than 1 percent of the annual crop of hellgrammites. Researchers concluded that the hellgrammite's secluded lifestyle offered protection against smallmouth predation. In other words, the insects were abundant, but not available—at least not to smallmouths. Rock bass, by contrast, consumed 13 percent of the hellgrammites.

It's not that smallmouths didn't *want* to eat hellgrammites. The insects' second greatest predator? Bait dealers. They accounted for 8 percent of the annual crop of hellgrammites (in 1983, that amounted to $100,000 worth!), selling them to none other than smallmouth bass anglers.

Smallmouths in the New River, in short, ate most of their hellgrammites while they were impaled on hooks. You won't see that one on the Discovery Channel.

For our purposes, the significance lies in the fact that hellgrammites are seldom encountered by smallmouths but are nevertheless highly desired—like truffles, as editor Jim Babb has noted. Researchers, in fact, noted that "total predation on hellgrammites may be slight due to their secretive behavior, and intraspecific competition may be a stronger regulator of populations . . . hellgrammites [in general] are not recognized as important prey for [smallmouths], but are used commonly for bait."

The more you think about it, the more that analysis makes sense. Over the years, I've caught a number of smallmouths on live hellgrammites in waters where they didn't—couldn't—exist, notably the Quabbin Reservoir (in fact, a bait store sells them to reservoir fishers) in Massachusetts, as well as Lake Ontario and Lake Champlain. The bass that took these hellgrammites had almost certainly never seen one before.

And while we see this pattern with earthworms and trout, it's unusual to see earthworm *imitations* work for trout the way hellgrammite imitations work for bass. It's as if we've been tempting smallmouths away from what they naturally eat with a glimpse of something they would like very much to eat, if only they could.

Hellgrammite imitations are fished using standard nymphing techniques: upstream, across stream, and across and down. Whatever your approach, it begins with identifying the current seams—those patches of slick water that run parallel to the heavy water. Midday bass like to hole up here in the shade of the boulders. The more realistic hellgrammite imitations are often a good choice when fished upstream on a dead drift; the swimmer types, such as the Murray's Hellgrammite, work well when manipulated, either with or into the current.

Presentation matters more than it should. I mean, you'd think that since smallmouths love 'em but can't catch 'em, they'd take hellgrammites no matter what. Were it that simple.

Three summers ago, I had a hellgrammite experience on the lower Miller's River in western Massachusetts that I guess you could call typical.

Twenty years ago the lower Miller's was one of those pieces of water too polluted and too warm for trout. These days, thanks to improved water quality, it's just too warm. The lower stretches are loaded with smallmouths of between 8 and 12 inches, with occasional bigger ones working their way up from the Connecticut River. The Miller's is noted for its good population of hellgrammites; not surprisingly, live hellgrammites account for the biggest bass every season.

My friend Steve Arneson knows the river well, and he agreed to show me his favorite stretch so that I could experiment with some new hellgrammite patterns.

We fished our way down through a long riffle, into some pocket water, and finally into a deep pool. My hot new imitation brought out a couple tiny bass that hung themselves on the swing, but that was it. To tell the truth I was a little disappointed—especially since Steve was working the water behind me and catching a number of fish on a floating Rapala.

He looked at my fly box. "I'd try one of those," he said, pointing at the brown-and-yellow streamer. "Browns and golds are good colors in here. I think that's why this gold Rapala works so well."

He was right. The streamer picked up a couple fish in the next run.

"We should head back," Steve said. "It's mostly flat water from here down to the Connecticut. We're far enough downstream now that we won't be back to the truck until two o'clock."

We sat on the bank in the shade. It was very hot, getting hotter.

"I'm surprised you didn't get anything on your hellgrammite fly," Steve said. "The river's loaded with them. Everyone uses them for bait."

"I know. Maybe I'll try it again on the way back up. Fishing upstream might be better."

I changed spools, switching to a floating line, and added some 3X tippet to the leader to bring it to around 7–8 feet. I left a 4-inch tag after tying on the tippet and crimped on a couple small split shot, tying an overhand knot below them. I tied on my hellgrammite imitation, lurched to my feet, and waded upstream to find some suitable water.

I found some, in a knee-deep run with a rocky bottom. The water got faster closer to midchannel, where it was waist deep. Part of the transitional strip was shaded. Steve had taken several fish from this stretch on the way down. If I would get a bass on a hellgrammite, it would be here.

My first cast landed at the head of the riffle. Partway through the drift the line twitched. I tightened up. Yes!

A smallmouth jumped in a spray of water and ran downstream into the deepest part of the pool, where it thumped and twisted on the bottom. At 13 inches it was a nice bass, dark olive like all the fish from this river, and I released it after a fun tussle. Finally.

It was very hot. I removed my hat, scooped up some river water, dumped it on my head. Steve was sitting over in the shade, sucking on a beer he'd stashed on the way down. He gave me the thumbs-up. I think he was cheering my fish.

I took several more smallmouths from that run, each one a bit smaller, and moved on to the next spot, which actually looked less productive. Three boulders, waist-high, with other smaller rocks scattered around, formed a tongue of current in a shallow area midriver. The sun pounded down. Steve sloshed across behind me, spinning rod over his shoulder; he collapsed in the shade and produced a second beer.

I made a cast, recovered the slack, and found a fish on my line. A 10-incher bounced its way down to me like a skipping stone. I released it, cast again to the same spot, and stood up on tiptoe to see the bottom. The substrate was sand-colored pebble. I watched the dark hellgrammite drifting against the lighter background. A shape floated out from the shade of the boulder and grabbed the fly in a flash of copper.

I landed that fish, and then caught six or seven fish on nearly successive casts. Saw the whole thing. It was terrific. Better than ESPN.

Arneson, who'd never before fly fished, or for that matter fly *cast*, waded out in his barn boots to give it a try. He thrashed around for a bit and buried a backcast in a tree branch half out of water behind us.

"Shit. What am I doing wrong.?"

"Try to keep your backcast a little higher." I waded back and unhooked his fly. And gave him some more room. I turned around just in time to see him hook his first fly-rod fish. He landed that one and caught another.

I sat on the bank, watching Steve and safeguarding his cache of beer. It felt good to see the fish respond to my hellgrammite imitation, though it was clear that the dead-drift approach was what was making the difference, not the particular fly pattern.

There was something else, too. No pattern or presentation, however inspired, can draw fish like catfish to a stinkbait. The smallmouths had gathered here, in this sun-drenched, ordinary slip of water, probably because it was also the *only* bit of feeding water within an entire wide, shallow, flat-water section of river. When a tasty-looking morsel like a hellgrammite came drifting into their sights, they weren't about to let it go by—even if they developed certain suspicions as their compatriots vanished into the great blue beyond. They really couldn't afford to, not if they wanted to survive in this highly competitive smallmouth environment, where forage of that size was clearly at a premium.

No one really knows about these things, but it's fun to speculate and, if nothing else, appreciate the complexity offered by smallmouth fishing. It's organized around opportunism rather than selectivity, and it really is quite interesting. To me, anyway.

As it turned out, I had quite a bit of time on my hands, with plenty of opportunity for such musings. Steve took more than a half-dozen fish, two of them close to a foot, and the little ones were still striking when we left after more than an hour. I didn't get in as much fishing as I would have liked.

8 Imitating Frogs, Mice, and Surface Minnows

As I've mentioned, much of my early smallmouth experience came on the St. Lawrence River. But that wasn't the only place I got to go bass fishing.

Until about age ten, I spent several weeks every summer in the Adirondacks visiting my great-aunt and -uncle. I managed to work in a few bass fishing trips up in the mountains, too.

This was during the 1950s and smallmouths and largemouths were replacing native brook trout in many Adirondack waters—a process that had been in progress for some time. Philistine that I was, I couldn't get those brookies out and bass in quickly enough. Bass was what I wanted. Bass.

There was still plenty of trout fishing around, however. It was no mean feat talking my Great-Uncle Frank, a lifelong brookie fisherman (he had raised my dad), into going bass fishing. But I was persistent. And he was very nice to me, to everyone really, a gracious gentleman—kind and old-fashioned, a man who wore a tie every day of his adult life, even when he went fishing.

Uncle Frank would often take me to a particular pond just outside of town that had smallmouths, sunfish, and bullheads. There were supposedly a few trout left in it, too. We fished from shore in the evening, and I caught plenty of bluegills and bullheads on worms by casting out into the black, still waters. At dusk, rises often appeared next to a patch of lily pads and reeds well out of casting range.

One evening I happened to look out to the lily pads just as a smallmouth leaped clear out of the water. It was the biggest bass I'd ever seen, and I did my best to stay inside my skin.

"Did you see that?" I yelled to Uncle Frank, who was fishing 50 feet or so down the shore.

He stuck his fly rod under his arm and held his hands far apart to indicate that he had. "He looked like an old socker," he called. "Probably after a frog!"

We never hooked that smallmouth, but I couldn't get it out of my mind. Brookies? No brookie could ever leap like that. Who in his right mind would bother with trout when there were fish like that to be caught? Fish that jumped clear into the air and ate frogs on their way back down.

No wonder smallmouth anglers like doing it with things that float on the surface and go *blip, pop,* and *gerblub.*

Unlike flies designed for other species that happen to catch bass (sometimes better than they catch the species they were designed for), poppers and bugs, as we have seen, were developed with bass in mind. Largemouths usually, but bass nevertheless. As such, they represent the only true "bass" flies, effective for largemouths as well as smallmouths. Dr. James Henshall, appropriately, designed and popularized the first one. For many people, fly fishing for smallmouths *means* poppers and bugs.

The bass don't always cooperate, of course. Summer surface fishing can be a waste of time on deep rivers, lakes, and reservoirs. In general, the more extensive the shallows in a given body of water, the more inclined smallmouths will be to feed on top. The best summer bug and popper fishing usually involves shallow ponds, midsized flows, and boulder-strewn rivers. Shorelines, grass beds, weed flats, and shoals are good spots to try—as long as the water remains shallow, say 5 feet deep.

By midsummer surface fishing may be limited to dawn and dusk. Rivers and flows can prove exceptions, however. Maine's Penobscot, Pennsylvania's Susquehanna, Minnesota's Boundary Waters, and Oregon's Umpqua—to name a few—may offer surface fishing all day long.

OF MICE AND FROGS

The enthusiasm smallmouths reserve for bugs seems far out of proportion to the amount of forage they actually get from the surface. When you think about it, the only food smallmouths would get from a lily pad or shoreline is the occasional frog or mouse that falls into the water. Yes, aquatic insects do hatch in still waters, and no doubt big *Hexagenia* and even caddis bring fish to the surface of some waters, but these account for relatively few meals when compared with crayfish and baitfish.

On most ponds, lakes, and slow-moving rivers, frogs are probably the most frequently consumed surface natural (at least for adult fish), and smallmouths may not eat as many of them as we think. Leopard frogs, for the most part, live in grass. If you have a cottage, you've probably noticed a point each summer when the frogs have "hatched" and are hopping about in the grass *near* the water. Frogs found *in* ponds are quite likely green frogs or bullfrogs.

As with hellgrammites, however, a certain prey can make an excellent bait or provide the basis for an effective imitation, even if bass seldom encounter it in the wild. And small leopard frogs make good baits; smallmouths snap them right up.

As for mice, smallmouths most certainly eat fewer of them than they do frogs. To tell the truth, smallmouths feed on mice mostly in magazine articles.

You know how the story goes. An old-timer ties a hook to a mouse, places it on a wood chip, and sets the chip adrift, only to pull the hapless creature off the chip as it reaches the hole with the big bass in it. He then, of course, promptly hooks the biggest bass in the river or pond.

This whole scenario seems increasingly improbable the more you think about it, the kind of thing that natives live to tell visiting sports. I mean, how do those arthritic old-timers manage to catch enough mice for a days' fishing? And how do they tie a line to a squealing mouse and keep the little bugger on a wood chip? I've yet to see a mouse harness, though I keep an eye out for them in the fishing catalogs.

In the end, smallmouths' desire to take these forage when they get the chance is what matters. And mice and frogs certainly elicit responses from opportunistic smallmouths.

As for imitations, hair-bodied mice are effective patterns. But I have a hard time imagining a situation in which a mouse bug would work and a Tapply Hair Bug wouldn't. A hatch of old-timers, maybe.

Explicit imitation probably matters more with frogs, not only in terms of offering a creamy olive belly color, but in terms of performance in the water. Leg action is the most important quality. As for size, try frogs a little on the large size, say size 2, 3X long—more for better hookups than for fish appeal.

I suppose it does make tactical sense to fish frog/mouse imitation bugs near the shoreline, where smallmouths are most likely to encounter real frogs and mice. Minnow imitations such as sliders, divers, and swimmers may be more useful over grass beds, midwater humps, and weed flats, where there is room for a retrieve; bass there are used to looking to the surface and seeing the streamlined shape of a minnow. On

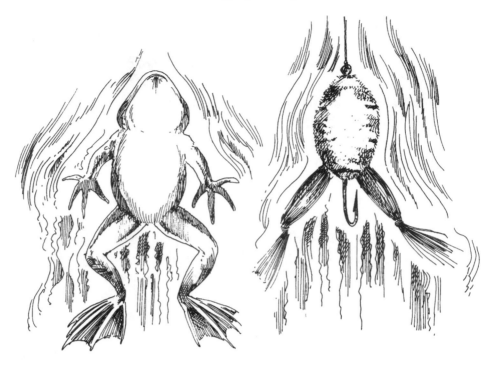

A real frog and a hair frog—from a smallmouth's viewpoint.

most days it probably doesn't matter, however, and I certainly don't change the type of bug I'm using for every different structure.

The above distinction actually works out very well as a fishing strategy, though. As most anglers know, the closer you can get your bug to cover, the better. Proximity is the key regardless of the composition of the cover—grass, weeds, rocks, boulders, trees, branches, or bridge abutments.

But along shorelines, a few feet of retrieve and often as not you're back out in open water. So the blunt-faced bugs that don't need much territory to work offer a clear advantage here. That's why rubber legs and marabou tails improve a bass bug: they provide a lot of action with little overall movement, letting you keep the bug in the sweet zone longer.

And that's also why the Gerbubble Bug, popularized in cork by Joe Brooks (as a largemouth fly) and in deer hair by Dave Whitlock, represents an excellent choice for this sort of fishing. Its hackle side feelers afford lifelike action with a minimum of bug movement.

Whatever bug or popper you choose, the basic manipulation involves a twitch so that it quivers as it drifts, and perhaps a gentle *pop*. In still water, the standard retrieve

Casting bugs to shoreline cover remains a popular and effective strategy for summer smallmouths. (Tony Zappia photo)

calls for resting the bug until the rings die out, then twitching it, then resting it for fifteen to twenty seconds. Then giving it a slight *pop*. I usually lose patience at this point and hustle it home.

Anglers who work bugs and poppers slowly probably catch a lot more bass than antsy types like me. But I've always thought that surface retrieves, in particular, should fit your temperament. The goal is to have fun, not give yourself an ulcer.

Most smallmouths, by the way, simply suck in the fly or bug, and most are missed because anglers strike too soon. If there is a secret to hooking them on poppers or bugs it is to wait until you actually see the bug disappear.

Like so many other fishing techniques that involve restraining instincts during a peak moment, this is easier said than done. Much.

Over the years, I've read a number of the-bass-weren't-biting-so-I-left-my-popper-out-while-I-ate-lunch-and-man-did-I-get-a-whopper stories. But it's never happened to me. The story does periodically cause me to slow down my bug fishing, just as stories about old-timers and mice leave me preferring gray bass bugs when fishing near brush-piles. To be honest, I don't know that either choice leads to any more smallmouths.

SURFACE MINNOW IMITATIONS

Now these are a different matter. When smallmouths are taking minnows near the surface, it may be important to imitate a baitfish—both in pattern and in presentation.

Marabou Muddlers or Dahlberg Divers skimmed through the surface film make the best surface minnow imitations. Cork sliders and Sneaky Petes do pretty well, too.

Smallmouths take these flies when they're twitched on top, although the signature retrieve, for the Dahlberg Diver anyway, has it diving then popping back to the top. Maybe I'm not doing it right. Most of my strikes come when the fly is swimming steadily just beneath the surface so that it pushes up a wake with its deer-hair collar.

The surface swimmer affords a lot of options, in other words, but you've got to *fish* it. It helps to stand up, which is one of the advantages boats have over canoes. A stripping basket can be a big help, too. The basket lets you retrieve in a steady, hand-over-hand, saltwater fashion, which in turn lets you keep the fly moving briskly so that it skims just beneath the surface.

If you're wading and there's some current, things get easier. In fact, fishing a surface swimmer in this fashion accounted for my first on-purpose, fly-caught smallmouth. So the technique has a special place in my heart.

As I said, while there wasn't a lot of bass sentiment in my family, there was considerable passion for fly fishing. My father taught me to catch trout on flies by the age of ten or eleven, and we went every weekend, and sometimes after supper on school nights. But that was mostly in the spring.

By July my dad was working at the state park, and I was trying my hand at the smallmouths in the waters of the St. Lawrence River. Later, in my teens, I spent my share of time drifting live bait across the broad shoals of Lake Ontario.

Over the years I came to love the warm breezes, the watercolor evenings, the expansive blue-green waters, as much as I did fly fishing for trout. Maybe more.

By age twenty-two I was basically a bass fisherman inside a trout fisherman's body, although I'd sublimated some of my urges by using deer-hair bugs (small ones, about size 8) for trout and by daydreaming about bugging for bass. I had little chance actually to do much of the latter, and my prospects didn't improve much after college, having landed a job in a Vermont hill town. Trout country.

The Lamoille, one of New England's finest trout waters, flowed through the village and occupied most of my fishing time my first summer there, the first summer I'd spent away from the shores of either Lake Ontario, the St. Lawrence River, or Lake Champlain. I missed the big water.

And I really missed the smallmouths.

A stripping basket is a welcome addition. (Tony Zappia photo)

I stopped into the local sports store, hoping for some word on the bass fishing. It wasn't the kind of thing you came right out and asked about, of course. You kind of worked up to it.

The owner, a slim, sunburnt man, sat slumped behind the counter. I asked him how the fishing was.

"Just got back from Arrowhead," he said—a reference to a reservoir on the lower Lamoille River near Milton. "All day long. One walleye, that's it. Frigging smallmouth bass kept hammering our lures, though. We wouldn't get fifty feet before one of them would grab a plug or a spinner."

Ah, the wild and wooly world of walleye trolling; the last thing you need is a fish that doesn't have enough sense to come into the boat once it's hooked.

"Those bass can be a real pain in the ass when you're trolling," I said.

"We had three lines out. They'd go jumping all over the place. We'd have to stop the boat, reel in the other lines, untangle everything. They're up in the Lamoille now, I hear it's loaded with them."

My right knee buckled, but I managed an indifferent sneer. "You mean that rocky shallow stretch between Georgia High Bridge and Fairfax?"

The guy looked at me funny. Then it was like a light went on in his head. Flatlander. He didn't say it; didn't have to.

"I mean so I don't waste my time trout fishing down there," I said quickly. "Jesus Christ, bass in the Lamoille. That's all we need."

It took me a good fifteen minutes to drive the 20 miles to that stretch of the river. Tarred roads wound down from the hills through the baked farmlands, and cows grazed on the hilly pastures.

Then the river came into view—wide, with gentle riffles and head-high boulders. It wasn't the bass water I was used to; no Champlain, no Ontario, no St. Lawrence. But it sure as hell wasn't trout water, either.

The water was warm, and I waded wet in sneakers, squishing out into the river, nearly falling twice, but flailing away nonetheless with streamers, wet flies, and hair bugs.

"Are you sure there's bass in here?" That's what a voice asked me.

I climbed to the top of a bleached boulder, looked into the pool, and spied several smallmouths scooting beneath the rocks. "Yup."

Back to frothing up the water. Nothing. "Damned bass."

Shadows edged out over the river, and the rises began, splashy ones at first and then, just before dark, full-bodied swirls. These had to be bass. But they wanted no part of the poppers.

I looked through my flies. "A black Marabou Muddler," I thought. "It's the only other bass thing I have that floats."

I cast for awhile, then, in resignation, held the fly downstream, still-fishing. It hung in the lip of the pool, made a wake in the silvery surface. I felt a nip, then another.

"Fallfish." I tried to hook one by dropping the fly back a couple inches, pulling it to the surface. "Missed him." I felt another nip, lifted the rod, and there was this 12-inch smallmouth skittering across the tail of the pool.

I caught three more smallmouths, breaking off a really nice one right at dark. The next evening, a black Marabou Muddler (this one tied with a body of black seal fur) produced a couple more bass. Other evenings, in the interests of science, I went wild and experimented with olive and brown; these colors worked, but not as well as black.

Like trout nymphs, the Muddler got better as it got chewed up. When the seal fur was about gone from the body, when the marabou was but a half-dozen ragged fibers— that's when the bass really went for it.

The smallmouths on the Lamoille were chasing minnows, plainly. Perhaps the black color offered a distinct outline against the lighter sky; the fishing was always best just before dark. I had my best luck by casting across and downstream and throwing a downstream mend in the line, which, in effect, caused the fly to accelerate a bit through the tail of the pool.

The whole thing left me with a bit of an attitude, I'm afraid. Let's call it "localized fly-fishing prowess." Not that anyone in northern Vermont gave a damn how many frigging bass I caught. For awhile I enjoyed the notoriety that comes with being a legend, even if it was in my own mind. But eventually I realized the limits of my achievement on the Lamoille.

As things have turned out, however, the strategy itself does have some general applications. The tail of a big pool, right where the water begins to funnel into a riffle, is an excellent spot to fish a surface swimmer in low light. The same goes for bigger rivers and grass beds, weed flats, and downed trees on the edges of the current. Perhaps minnows gather there to take small midges; perhaps they lose their hold in the slack water and get caught in the strengthening current. Either way, smallmouths don't pass up such spots, and neither should anglers.

FLOAT TRIPS

Surface streamers are particularly useful flies for float fishing. Shallow weed beds and shoreline cover are prime spots because they hold schools of minnows. Often as not I tie on a surface streamer like a Marabou Muddler or Dahlberg Diver when we're shoving off and leave it on till we beach the canoe at night.

You cast as you float, fishing ahead of the boat or canoe. The fish don't see you first that way, and—more important—you have more control over your streamer. You can fish it more slowly, make it dart instead of drag.

Most big rivers have some "bottomless" holes of 50 feet or more, and they look like really sexy places to fish.

Ignore them.

You'll find resting fish, if any. With a fast-sink line and streamer, you might hook a walleye or a rock bass.

Some of the biggest smallmouths feed on baitfish in shallow water. Look for them alongside boulders, blowdowns, and shaded banks. Actively feeding fish often seek out more subtle "structures," like small weedlines, current breaks, and transitions in the stream bed. And they tend to be shallower than many people think. Weedy islands or shoals that appear in midstream make particularly good spots in late summer and early fall, when young-of-the-year baitfish school there.

These are all good spots to explore with a surface swimmer or a hair bug. Personally, I find a nice resonance between canoe floating and surface fishing. If nothing else, you get to try a lot of different places. As noted earlier, the first cast into a spot often produces the biggest smallmouth; when you float-fish you have the opportunity to make "first casts" all day.

Hair bugs and surface swimmers let you see the proceedings. And float-fishing only heightens the excitement, with the time-suspended sense it evokes. You never know what might be waiting around the bend.

I remember a float trip on the Grasse River, a northern New York tributary of the St. Lawrence, with my friends Tony Zappia and George Dodge. We came upon a weedy shoal in midriver and began taking smallmouths with floating Rapalas and Dahlberg Divers.

The action picked up toward dusk, with bluegills snapping at the surface and an occasional bigger smallmouth showing in the half-light.

Suddenly a wake appeared behind my fly. "Must have hooked a weed," I thought. But the wake grew in size and closed on my fly, engulfing it in a fierce, boatside swirl.

The fish steamed off across the creek, my fly reel chattering. I felt like I'd a hooked a goddamn ferry boat.

"Muskie!" Tony and George called in unison.

Then the line fell slack and line, leader, and fly all came back intact. "That fish never even knew it was hooked," said George.

We still had a half mile to float before we'd reach Tony's truck. It was nearly dark now, with the September sun tucked behind the Adirondack foothills. And it was quiet, too. Tony and George cast Rapalas and landed several nice smallmouths as we drifted.

I mostly sat in the bow and watched the black water slip beneath the boat. Never before had I hooked a muskie on a fly rod, and it was nice to sit there and just think for a while.

9 *Imitating Baitfish*

The seventy-five year popularity of feathered minnows tells us that, among other things, anglers have long understood the advantages of flies that imitate baitfish. No news flash here.

Baitfish are a smallmouth staple. They sustain adult bass from ice-out to ice-in and occasionally during the winter months. It comes as little surprise that streamers can be fished effectively throughout the season.

Much of the earliest streamer fishing involved trolling, and that remains an effective strategy today—not only for the salmonids that inspired early streamer developments, but for smallmouth bass as well.

Which brings to mind a fishing trip years ago in Wells, New York, in the big woods of the Adirondacks. I arrived at my friend Pete Bellinger's house, and we looked out at the silver surface of Algonquin Lake.

"No trout," Pete said, reading my thoughts. "But we've been getting some smallmouths. Let's go before it gets dark. We can take the canoe."

"Don't have any bass bugs with me. Just trout flies," I said. "And some streamers."

"That's all you'll need," he said, easing into the canoe.

Pete had a Gray Ghost attached to the end of his spinning rod, so I opened my streamer book and plucked from the fleece my favorite streamer, a Nine-three. We hung them off the canoe and began trolling along the shore, within a rod length of the bushes.

As dusk settled, bats fluttered out of the heavy growth, flitting about our canoe.

"You troll pretty close to shore, huh?"

"That's where the bass are," Pete laughed.

I was about to point out that's where the bats were as well when Pete hooked a smallmouth. Five minutes later I landed its twin. We had dinner before we finished our first pass of the lake.

The smallmouths weren't large—two pounds was tops—but catching them this way, near the surface from a canoe, made them seem bigger. Pete used his light spinning rod and 6-pound test, which did just as well as my fly rod, floating line, and 9-foot leader. The trick was to drag a long line without weight and keep the canoe close to the bank and the canopy of alders. The smallmouths had moved in to feed on the baitfish that had left the bottom to chase insects.

We'd fished here back in the mid-1970s, so it has been twenty years. But the fishing was not easy to forget.

We'd paddle through the mountain dusk. Paddle, glide, paddle. Wedge the rod against the bottom of the canoe; hold it there with the backside of your foot. Pluck the line to give the streamers a twitch. Then try to forget about the rod—until it rattles to life against your ankle. Fish on!

Drop the paddle. The rod, grab the rod! Look back and the bass springs out of the water, again and again and again.

BAITFISH AS FORAGE

Any of the following can be smallmouth forage: shiners, chubs, dace, suckers, smelts, stonerollers, darters, sculpins, madtoms, fingerling bullheads, and juvenile panfish and gamefish. Cannibalism is common. Contrary to popular opinion, however, smallmouths do not appear to be serious predators on juvenile salmonids, as a long-term study on the Columbia River indicated—most likely because juvenile salmonids and adult smallmouths occupy different habitats.

Members of the minnow family (Cyprinidae), particularly the genus *Notropis,* which includes baitfish such as the emerald shiner and silver shiner, are among the most important forage. Other studies have found minnows in the genera *Luxillus,* which includes the common shiner, and *Cyprillae* to be significant, too. In rivers and streams, members of the genus *Campostoma,* or stonerollers, can be important prey, as a 1984 study of Missouri's Current River and its tributaries indicated.

Smallmouths often feed on Percidae, in particular younger members of the genus *Perca,* or yellow perch, as established by studies done on Oneida Lake in New York in

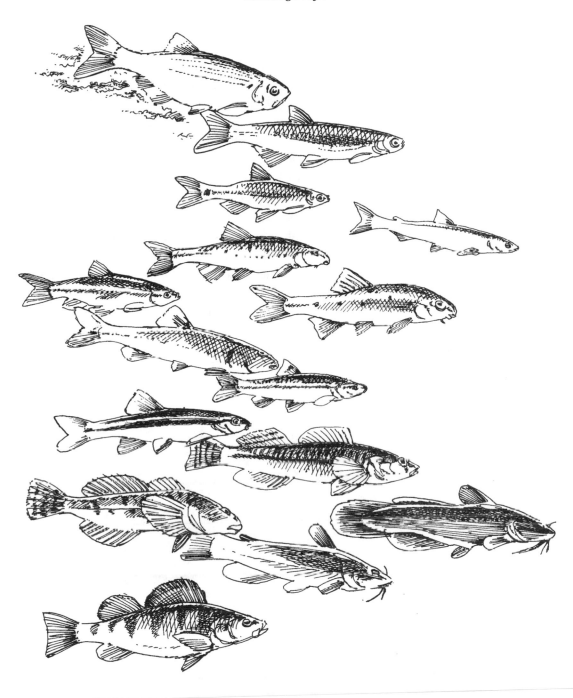

Baitfish: from top to bottom, alewife, two shiners, smelt, three suckers, stonerollers, chub, dace, darter, sculpin, madtom, fingerling bullhead, and juvenile panfish.

1954, Canadarago Lake in New York in 1978, and Neshoba Lake in Wisconsin in 1983. Members of the genus *Percina,* or darters, constitute a significant forage, too. In fact, smallmouths seem especially partial to them when they can get them. I've yet to encounter a study or a situation in which these forage were present in any numbers and failed to hold a special appeal for smallmouths.

Alewives were found to comprise a major proportion of the smallmouth's diet in Webster's 1954 study of Cayuga Lake in New York. Subsequent studies on Oneida Lake and on the Great Lakes reached similar conclusions. Madtoms (*Noturus*) and, in particular, sculpins (Cottidae) can also be important in rivers and streams.

Predictably, it usually comes down to which baitfish are most abundant and available. In summer, smallmouths may shift their interest if crayfish become more abundant and available. If crayfish are not present, smallmouths stay with baitfish throughout the year.

A certain selective opportunism may come into play in the interaction of smallmouths and baitfish. That is, smallmouths may feed extensively on certain baitfish, yet remain on the lookout for more desirable forage and take that whenever the opportunity presents itself. Perch and darters exemplify this dynamic. In the 1978 study on Canadarago Lake in New York, smallmouths fed extensively (up to 75 percent of forage) on perch—as did the lake's largemouths and pickerel. Smallmouths also took

Darters, like this logperch, are preferred forage for smallmouths everywhere. Note the tubular shape and mottled coloration.

darters (up to 20 percent of their forage some years); the other predators, however, showed no such predilection.

Some studies report that smallmouths select for size before species, particularly in streams and rivers, where smallmouths have little choice but to eat whatever species they can catch. As one researcher admitted, "Fish of any species in the same waters as the bass may be eaten at the appropriate size." Opportunists, indeed.

What about the old saw, Bigger bait, bigger bass? By and large, it's true. Admittedly, there are some instances of adult smallmouths feeding on very small forage fish. For example, one study showed that bass began feeding on perch fry as early as June 9 (smallmouth spawning was just ending), when the fry were 10–15mm long. But research generally supports the notion that bigger bass prefer bigger minnows.

The study, conducted on the Current River in Missouri, identified more than twenty-five species of prey fish that "have an adult size usable as prey. . . ." The researchers found it hard to pick the most popular, noting, "We know, however, that there was an abundant and diverse cyprinid (minnow) population and that predators selected certain sizes from those available." Certain sizes usually meant bigger. The mean length of seined prey fish was 45mm, and the mean length of prey fish eaten by rock bass was 47mm. But the mean length of prey species eaten by smallmouths was nearly double those sizes—80mm, or approximately 3¼ inches.

The conclusion? Adult smallmouths generally ate larger prey fish—but did not ignore smaller ones.

Some evidence suggests that, as adult bass grow, they change their prey, feeding on the biggest baitfish. The Columbia River study, for instance, found that "crayfish were the single most important food in the diet of smallmouth bass less than 250 mm long, but prickly sculpin were the most important prey of fish 250–399 mm long (31%–49%). Suckers were the most important food (52%) of smallmouth bass greater than 400 mm." While much of the baloney you hear about big bait–big fish is just that, in the case of baitfish and smallmouths it seems as true as these things get.

In short, the pattern seems to go as follows: Smallmouths feed on baitfish throughout the year, although during midsummer, young-of-the-year baitfish may be too small, while crayfish become abundant and available. In waters without crayfish, baitfish abundance can lead to predation all summer, with one prey species—such as the perch or alewife—dominating the diet. Smallmouths can show a loose preference for certain baitfish, whether darters and sculpins, or soft-finned species such as alewife, shad, shiner, chub, dace, and sucker. Size is important, and that usually means bigger rather than what is most abundant. The bigger the bass, the more likely this is to be true.

IMITATING BAITFISH

The streamers and bucktails that became so popular with trout anglers in the twentieth century had a tougher time establishing themselves with smallmouth fishers.

Most anglers preferred the spinner-and-fly combination, probably more out of intuition than imitation. In 1953, McClane noted that not only does the spinner get the fly down to where the fish are, but—with the fly at the rear—it does a good job of imitating a minnow.

Not all anglers saw it that way. What I got from my Uncle Frank was that the spinner held a smallmouth's attention until it saw the food at the end. He never said anything about minnows.

At any rate, the spinner-and-fly caught a lot of bass, and it remains an excellent choice, as Tim Holschlag explains in his fine book on stream smallmouths. But there's also a dimension to the spinner-and-fly that seems out of place in the modern age of Flashabou, glittering eyes, and High-D lines. In effect, its archetype has jumped the median and ended up in the plastic tackle boxes of spin fishers and bait casters in the form of Roostertails and spinner baits.

In this age of forage-based imitations, fly fishers often focus on matching streamers as precisely as possible to the baitfish in the water. Impressive as it is, this level of imitation may well be lost on the bass.

Smallmouths often take baitfish in a rush, quite unlike their deliberate manner of taking crayfish or their delicate method of sucking in drifting nymphs. They seem more to respond to certain baitfish triggers that elicit a predator response than to scrutinize the extent to which a streamer replicates a baitfish.

Identifying these triggers and capitalizing on them in pattern and presentation might just be the most important thing a streamer stripper can do.

THE WAY THEY LOOK

Nearly all my smallmouth streamers are between size 6, 4X and size 2, 8X, with size 4, 4X–6X a standard.

As for shape, the traditional streamer pattern suggests the outline of the shiner, sucker, chub, and dace side of minnow life (the Marabou Muddler has a distinctive head, which some anglers prefer). In those lakes and reservoirs where bass key on shad and alewives, there may be some advantage to streamers with broad profiles, typical of Whitlock's shad imitations, Matukas, and Zonkers.

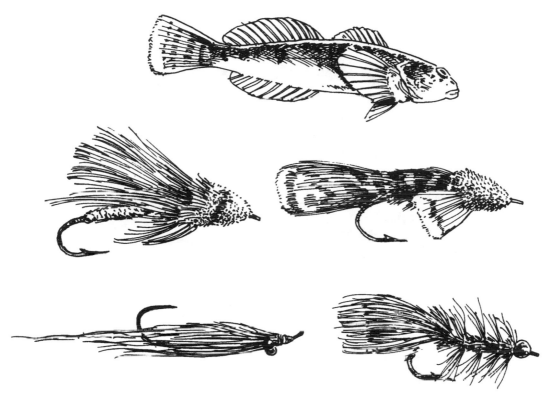

Sculpin with its imitations: Marabou Muddler, Woolly-beaded Sculpin, Clouser Foxee, and Bead-bead Woolly Bugger.

In bigger rivers, where madtoms, sculpins, and darters comprise important forage, the distinct profile of a Woolly-headed Sculpin pattern or old hunt-headed standards like Muddler Minnows and Marabou Muddlers could constitute a trigger of sorts, particularly in fast water where bass depend on a brief glimpse of shape. If you want to put an extra-fine point on this matter of shape, a darter's tubular body is probably better represented by a Bead-head Woolly Bugger than by the flat-headed design of sculpin and madtom imitations.

Most anglers believe that eyes are an important trigger, particularly on big-eyed forage such as alewives. I put eyes on my streamers, too, though I'm not sure how much it matters. I like what expert Maine fly tyer Danny Legere said about this question. Legere was referring to landlocked salmon streamers a few years back when it was tough to get jungle cock for a reasonable price, but I think his point holds for streamer eyes in general.

"No doubt about it," he said. "Jungle cock eyes dress off a streamer fly nicely. But it's not like we stopped catching fish because we ran out of jungle cock."

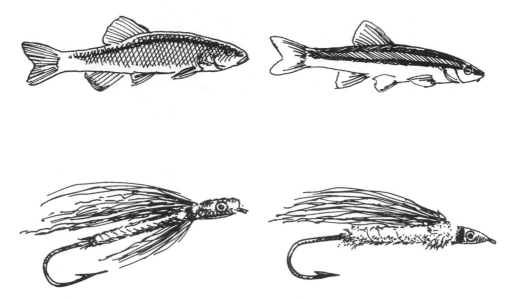

Chubs and dace and their imitations: Marabou streamer and Thunder Creek–style marabou streamer.

Color and flash, on the other hand, are very important considerations for small-mouths—in my opinion, the most important appearance "triggers" in a streamer fly. The best colors for streamers follow the general principle of matching color pattern to water stain noted in chapter 4.

For marabou streamers, the white wing–silver body is probably the top combination for clear water. I add eyes, Flashabou, and a darker color on top to keep things interesting. The Clouser Deep Minnow in chartreuse and white is an excellent general choice for reasonably clear water. The Clouser Ultra Deep Minnow, with a light-colored, translucent wing and plenty of sparkle, makes an excellent choice in very clear water.

A yellow-and-brown marabou wing with a gold body is a top combination for stained water. The Clouser Foxee Minnow, with a brown wing and bright orange eyes, is an excellent choice, too.

Although it's important to keep these color patterns in mind, they afford starting points. I fish some waters where yellow/gold/brown/black works well, for instance, but only when tied with a great deal of white in the wing. Interestingly, these waters have broad-shaped forage—young-of-the-year shad and golden shiners (which aren't as golden as they sound). Perhaps the fish are keyed into broad, light-colored flash.

And I can think of other waters where dace are a preferred forage, and the most important trigger is not so much color or flash but a peacock herl sword running the length of the pattern suggesting, I've always thought, the emerald stripe on the side of the baitfish. Perhaps the smallmouths use the direction of the stripes (lateral as opposed to vertical) to distinguish dace from perch.

My favorite forage-based color trigger is mottled brown—whether in the wing of a muddler, in wound-on grouse hackle, or in mottled marabou (available from Umpqua Feather Merchants). I think this color trigger does an excellent job of imitating darters and sculpins (and probably mayfly nymphs, stonefly nymphs, and crayfish, too). It seems particularly effective in rivers.

Smallmouths, interestingly, often differ from other gamefish in their color preferences. White is by far the best streamer color for smallmouths on Lake Champlain, for instance, while dark-colored, featherwing streamers are the most popular choices for landlocked salmon. Champlain angler Shawn Gregoire attributes the difference to the fact that the salmon feed on smelts, the bass on shiners. Perhaps. At any rate, the strong color separations that appear so important in smelt-imitating streamers for salmon and trout appear lost on smallmouths.

THE WAY THEY ACT

Bob Clouser puts it well: It's not so important how closely a fly imitates a natural forage. It just has to act like one. Harry Murray makes a similar point in his book, noting that it's not just how streamers look that matters, it's how they act in the water, too.

Different types of streamers have different actions, of course, which have to match not only with the forage, but also (and generally more importantly) with how and where you are fishing.

Start, for instance, with fly fishing in fairly shallow (under 10 feet) flowing water, where sculpins and darters and other bottom-oriented species are top forage. For my money, it's tough to beat the action of a Bead-head Woolly Bugger. The bead head keeps the fly near the bottom, and the hackle fibers and marabou tail provide the action with a minimum of movement. The fly moves within itself and stays within a matter of inches of the bottom, which is what you want in a sculpin/darter imitation.

The Clouser Foxee is a good sculpin/darter imitation here, too. So is a weighted Marabou Muddler. Stiff-winged sculpin imitations, which offer a stronger profile, can't match marabou for action in slow or medium currents. They may be better choices in quick, shallow water, where the prime presentation is an up-and-across dead drift and the bass may be keying on a shape whisking by.

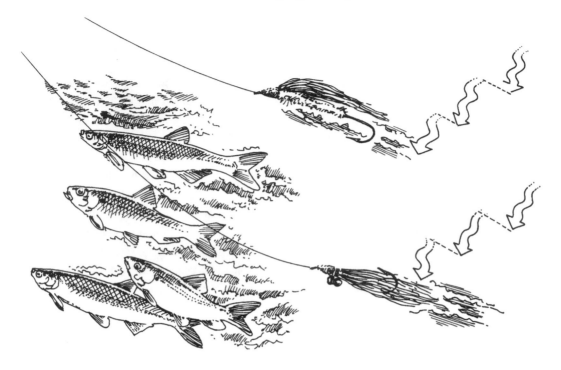

Deep-water baitfish, with Marabou Matuka and Clouser Minnow (fished with a strip/pause retrieve).

Chubs, suckers, sculpins, baby bullheads, and other bottom-oriented forage often tip up and down, with noses on the bottom and tails high. The Clouser Minnow and Bead-head Woolly Buggers offer reasonable imitations of this behavior, too.

The standard marabou streamers or Marabou Muddlers make good imitations of mid-depth baitfish such as chubs, dace, and shiners. In waters less than 10 feet deep, the Thunder Creek marabou (see appendix C) is a great producer. This pattern really depends upon a horizontal retrieve, however. It loses action when the body of the fly is weighted and fished up and down, because the marabou just wraps around the hook.

Deeper, bigger water is home to soft-finned cyprinids, alewives, and shad. The challenge facing the fly fisher comes less in the form of imitating the forage and more in the form of making imitations work like minnows at extreme depths. In general, the deeper the fishing, the slower the presentation—there's simply no way around it—and the more the action has to come from the fly itself.

Which, in a nutshell, is the genius of the Clouser Minnow. Standard marabou patterns also work quite well when weighted (unlike feathered streamers). The action is all in the wing, and a contrastingly heavy body actually improves their action.

For deeper-water fishing when the body of the streamer is weighted, the Matuka style makes even better sense: With the fibers of the feathers (I again prefer marabou) coming out of the top of the fly, it is at its best when falling. The weighted Matuka, in other words, is meant to be fished vertically. It can be used with a strip-pause-strip pattern in water 7–10 feet deep, but its real significance begins once you get below 10 feet.

Again, this is really putting a fine point on things. I like tying flies and experimenting with different patterns. Often as not a straight marabou or Marabou Muddler does just fine in deep water. The general marabou or Marabou Muddler could well be the most important streamer in your box.

The important point is that different materials respond differently to current and water pressure. Traditional feathered patterns such as the Nine-three or Gray Ghost come alive in the current of rivers or when trolled, but they suffer if weight is added because the action emerges from the movement of the entire fly, not just the wing. If weight is necessary, add some split shot a couple feet above the fly.

The action inherent in a fly type is only one influence on how it ultimately behaves. It matters quite a bit how the individual at the helm is handling the matter.

And, as it turns out, how a fly behaves can have a surprising influence on whether a smallmouth strikes.

OPTIMAL PREY BEHAVIOR

Much—perhaps too much—of fly-fishing attention focuses on how gamefish respond to baitfish. There's another side to the story. Smallmouths often strike or fail to strike based on what the prey does. It certainly makes sense to have prey imitations behave in the way that is most likely to trigger a strike.

Recent research has shed some light on this matter. One study looked at how the presence of an additional prey (a crayfish) influenced the escape strategies of prey (a sculpin) confronted with a smallmouth bass.

Five sculpins were placed in a tank, which had a hiding spot in the middle. A smallmouth of between 10 and 12 inches was released into the tank. The sculpins "froze" in their places. It didn't work. The smallmouth spotted them, swam over, and began picking them off.

For comparison the test was duplicated (each of these tests was in fact duplicated numerous times) with ten crayfish in the tank, and their presence changed things. The sculpins made more extensive use of the hiding spot, and only about one in four were eaten; when crayfish weren't present, the bass got nearly half of the sculpins.

The crayfish themselves were too big (1¾–2½ inches!) to be a prime forage—only 4 out of 240 were eaten during the experiment.

Perhaps, researchers speculated, the sculpins sensed the smallmouth's presence more quickly from the reaction of the crayfish. Perhaps the crayfish distracted the bass (the smallmouths would show an initial interest, but the crayfish would wave their chelae at them and the smallmouths would back off), and the sculpins used the instant to make a break for cover. At any rate, with crayfish present most of the sculpins made a break for the hiding spot, and all of these made it. One or two sculpins tried the old "freezing" strategy. Guess what happened to them?

The description of the actual feeding behavior is quite interesting:

> Although sculpin seemed (to us) to be better camouflaged (against the sand-gravel substrate) than crayfish, bass apparently had little trouble detecting sculpin. Bass attacks on sculpin usually consisted of a swim across the pool culminating in prey capture in one continuous movement. Sculpin showed little escape or defensive response to bass attacks. Because the sculpin showed neither effective avoidance (refuge use) nor escape behavior, predation rates were relatively high.

This brings up numerous questions about the assumptions behind accepted fishing strategies. First to come under scrutiny is the notion that bright colors are good because the fish have a tough time seeing under certain conditions. Smallmouth eyesight seemed just fine in this case. Perhaps even more significant was the smallmouths' propensity for taking the least challenging prey, passing up not only fierce 2-inch crayfish but speeding sculpins as well. They ate only the sculpins that tried to blend into the background. Perhaps, too, the study explains why smallmouths take baitfish in a rush: They may have the best chance if they strike *before* the baitfish are aware of their presence.

Smallmouths have to do something to be good foragers, because they actually appear quite inefficient. They can't dig in the stones like a rock bass; they can't close the last 5 yards in a burst of speed like a northern, with its large rear fins and broad tail; they're not streamlined and built for cruising like a trout. And they don't ambush from cover like a largemouth. So what they do is swim in schools and try to catch open-water baitfish unaware, cornering them against a ledge if they have to. Not that they won't chase a baitfish; they will. Foraging in schools, however, allows one bass to intercept a bait fleeing from another. They help each other out, in other words, or else there would be no advantage to the schooling.

Whenever possible, a smallmouth would just as soon take a baitfish (and probably a crayfish, too) before it realizes it is being sized up. Abundant *and* available, in other words.

If there is a starting point to executing any smallmouth retrieve, it is here.

Marabou Muddler/sculpin imitations work in a variety of situations across smallmouth range.

RETRIEVES

There are a number of standard retrieves, and many combinations therein. The first is the strip-pause-strip. Clouser recommends a strip as soon as the streamer hits the water. After that, pause, Clouser notes, and get ready, because smallmouths often take on the drop. Clouser's instructions fit with the underwater observations of Paul Johnson, who explains that fish often show the most interest upon the lure or fly's initial forward movement.

The strip-pause-strip retrieve also clearly fits with the smallmouth's attraction to an unsuspecting prey. Because smallmouths usually take streamers in a rush, the pause can be just the ticket. The strip-pause-strip retrieve is particularly important in lakes and ponds, where depth can be controlled by how long you wait before starting the retrieve and in turn by how long you wait on each pause. The advantages of the weighted Marabou Matuka come clearly into play here, as the marabou, which comes out of the top on a Matuka tie, often works best when the fly is pausing (sinking).

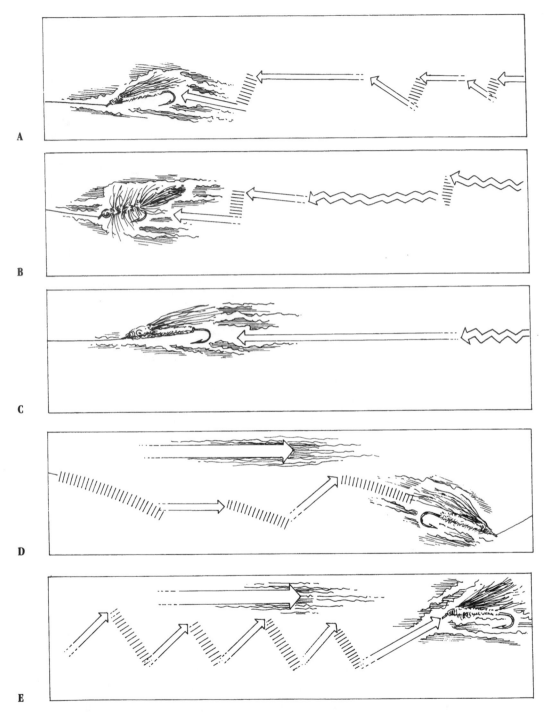

A) a strip-pause retrieve; B) 2- to 3-inch strips, with occasional pauses; C) swimming retrieve (fast two-handed stripping); D) streamer drifting with the boat, and occasional weak twitches to imitate baitfish fighting to stay upright; E) controlled downstream drift with an occasional twitch to imitate an escaping minnow.

The second retrieve consists of 2- to 3-inch strips, with occasional pauses. You can vary the speed, and with an unweighted streamer this brings about an effective darting motion. This retrieve can be particularly effective with feathered streamers. With a weighted fly, it brings out a more erratic action. With the Bead-head Woolly Bugger or Clouser Minnow, it gives it a hopping action across the bottom.

Third is the swimming retrieve, which can best be executed saltwater style; that is, with a stripping basket (desirable whenever you fish in a boat, but quite essential for this retrieve). Stick the rod under your arm and retrieve the fly hand over hand, feeding the coils of line into the basket.

At times, a steady swimming retrieve can be just the ticket for hard-fished small mouths in clear water. Usually slow is better, but not always. The hand-over-hand retrieve lets you concentrate on swimming your fly at a particular pace in a way that's impossible when you have a fly rod in one hand. I don't knit, but I have a feeling people who do know what I mean.

The fourth retrieve, a controlled drift with an occasional twitch to give the impression of an escaping minnow, uses the boat drift to swim the fly. This retrieve works very well with a floating Muddler Minnow, with a marabou streamer in mid-depths, or with a sculpin/darter imitation right near the bottom.

The fifth retrieve is not really a retrieve at all; in fact, it involves paying out line, all the while twitching the rod tip. Again, a drifting boat is necessary. Try to give the impression of a baitfish fighting to stay upright and losing the battle.

One day last summer, as an example, my friend Stan Warner and I were fishing the Connecticut River, on the upriver stretches where it winds through the farmland of northern New England. We'd anchored in a rocky section in 10 feet of water. Recent rains and upriver dam releases had the current pushing pretty well.

My crayfish pattern turned up nothing, but Stan caught several smallmouths in the 2- to 3-pound class on live shiners by still-fishing the baits downriver. Crayfish imitations fish poorly with such a presentation, anyway—they tend to spin in the current—so I changed to a streamer and flipped it out beside the boat, then stripped off line and let the streamer sink as it drifted downriver. The current was strong enough that when I held the streamer in one spot it would ride off the bottom. Then I'd let it drop back a couple feet, hold it there, work it ahead in gentle rod twitches. I kept this up for quite awhile.

Suddenly I felt a solid weight—a good fish! I let the slack line slip through my fingers in rubbery jerks until I got the fish on the reel. It was a nice smallmouth—nearly 16 inches, my best fish of the day.

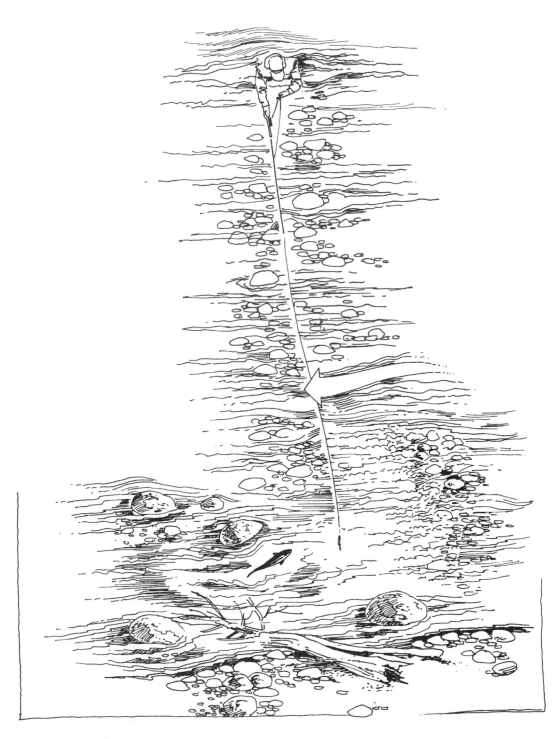

Swimming a streamer across a stream can be an excellent strategy for taking bass lying behind boulders or holding at the merging of a riffle and pool.

There were only a couple of turns of line left on my reel, incidentally, when that fish took. And I'd started the backward drift right at the boat. It would be nice to write that I changed to a streamer, made a single cast, and hooked the best fish of the day. But that wouldn't be true to the spirit of the incident. It *was* my first cast. But I was about fifteen minutes into it.

PRESENTATION

Matching presentation to water type may well be the most important aspect of streamer-fishing for smallmouths—whether it's a stream, a big river like the Connecticut, a pond, or, as we'll see in chapters 11 through 13, one of the largest waterways in the nation.

First, streams and rivers. You can fish the bass that lie in the shade of boulders by working a streamer across the stream, though be sure to cast well above the target spot. Often smallmouths will take on the drift. Those fish holding at the merging of the riffle and pool can also be tempted with an across-stream approach. The strip-pause-strip retrieve works well here.

You might find that streamers work well when cast upstream, too. Try using a strip retrieve, twitching the streamer back with the current. You can also cast upstream and

Two-handed retrieve in use—rod under angler's arm, line going hand over hand into a stripping basket belted around waist.

across, mend the line to get some depth, and then swim (saltwater style or with 2- to 3-inch strips) the streamer back across the stream. This is an excellent technique with the Thunder Creek tie, by the way.

Smallmouths seem to respond well to a strip-pause-strip retrieve in slack water or, where there is a bit of current, to a bottom-brushing drift, particularly if you fish it on a downstream swing in Leisenring-lift fashion. The Bead-head Woolly Bugger can be an excellent choice here, and so can a weighted marabou. When the streamer finally does make it across the current and swings below you, let it hang there awhile like a struggling minnow. This can be effective in all depths, by the way, from the surface to the bottom of deeper pools.

You can use the same techniques fishing in a boat. Streamers are great for float trips when the fish are not on the surface—in breezy weather, for instance. Shallow weed beds and shoreline cover make prime spots since they hold schools of minnows. This is shallow-water fishing, for the most part, calling for a horizontal presentation. Thunder Creeks, unweighted marabous, feathered streamers—all do the trick. Sometimes a microshot placed a foot or so up on the tippet will let you effect an erratic retrieve without burying the fly in the weeds.

Streamers can be used effectively in still water, too, with shorelines a fruitful if obvious place to begin. The smaller the pond or lake, the better the shoreline fishing—at least that's been my experience. You can troll, as Pete and I did on Algonquin Lake, but you can also cast streamers productively, too, especially when boulders or fallen timber punctuate the shoreline and rule out trolling tight to the bank.

Standard practice involves drifting along and casting toward the bank (in effect, parallel to the protruding cover). While a canoe may be more aesthetically pleasing, a boat definitely makes retrieving subsurface flies easier. Whatever your choice, let the motion of the drifting craft help control the line so that you sort of drift/troll the streamer through the water.

You can work ahead of the boat, too, as we will see in chapter 12. Like fishing upstream, presenting the fly ahead of the boat lets you not only avoid initial drag, but also deliver the fly a lot deeper with less weight. If you work at it, you can actually maintain *more* control over the position and the action of your streamer, as with any other sort of upstream presentation.

Minnows spend much of their time in the grass, and the smallmouths move in to find them. The trick is to find breaks in the weeds; gravel pockets with scattered boulders are ideal. If there are no gravel patches or bare spots, look to the edges of the weed beds for the weedline. This is a great place to drift/troll feathered streamers or to fish marabous with a strip-pause-strip retrieve. Match the material of the streamer to

This smallmouth took a Nine-three, an excellent traditional streamer.

the speed of boat movement—feathered streamers for a fast drift, marabous for poking along.

There's more to smallmouth fishing than shorelines. If anything, in fact, fly fishers spend too much time there. On many smallmouth waters, the best summer fishing is found on offshore shoals and bars, and streamers have a place here as well, as we will see in chapters 11, 12, and 13.

For now, these are the principles, as I see them, of fishing streamers for smallmouths. Fishing offshore and deep water involves modifications, some different approaches. These spots can be well worth it, particularly during the fall, when bass gorge on minnows.

In the meantime we have crayfish, the forage that dominates summer smallmouth fishing. In the biggest waters, crayfish occur in such numbers that the bass can afford to be selective for them. But they're highly desirable forage for opportunistic smallmouths in smaller waters, too.

Not that baitfish cease being important. Periodically throughout the summer on the broad shoals of big lakes, and on rivers and flows, streamer fishing emerges as a singularly effective smallmouth technique. It most certainly returns in fall with renewed energy as the bass build energy reserves for winter.

We'll be back.

10 *Imitating Crayfish*

During the summer, crayfish are the forage of choice for smallmouths. The more you know about crayfish and how to fish their imitations, the more and bigger bass you will catch. Few things about smallmouth fishing can be put so simply and with such certainty.

My own introduction to crayfish came when I was a boy at Cedar Point State Park on the St. Lawrence River. As I described earlier, after learning to catch smallmouth bass on minnows I'd come to think of myself as a pretty good fisherman. Then the bass stopped biting.

"Why don't you ask Don how he's catching them?" my dad suggested, referring to Don Wolfe, the park caretaker and smallmouth guru.

Yeah, why not? It had worked before.

The next morning I found Don working with some other men, laying pipe on a cedar-ringed knoll that overlooked the river. It was hot, and they shoveled steadily, shining with sweat. I waited until they took a break before walking over.

Tall, covered with grime, Don hung on his shovel, drawing deeply on a cigarette. The smoke curled around him like incense.

Don had poor vision and wore glasses all the time. When he looked at you, he zeroed in, craning his neck, focusing his pale blue eyes. It reminded me of stories I'd read of bears, how they couldn't see you from a distance, but once they located you they never took their eyes off you. I was in his sights now, and I stepped forward.

"Having any luck? I'm not catching much at all except for rock bass. I got one keeper all week," I said, grabbing a breath. "And I've been fishing out to the island every day."

Don peered down at me over his glasses. "What are you using for bait?" he asked. "Shiners, worms."

"Come here," he said, and I followed him down the dock to his drab olive duck boat. He knelt on the dock, then pulled in his bait bucket and flipped open the tin lid. Inside, clusters of crayfish clung to the sides and peered up at us.

"Here's what you want," Don said. He picked one up, rotated it. "Hook him through the tail and pinch off his claws. Otherwise he'll grab the bottom and screw up the drift on you. Fish him just like a minnow. The bass will grab him and run. Let him go for a little way before you set the hook."

"You got a bait bucket at your boat?" he continued. "Here, hold out your hands."

Won't they pinch? flashed across my mind, but I was no whiny-ass tourist.

Don scooped out a dozen or so crayfish and dropped them into my cupped hands. I hustled them over to my boat and dumped them into my pail. Their scuttling made scratching sounds on the tin walls. A little moss and water and things quieted down.

When I reached the shoal off Linda Island the next morning, the water surface lay still. It was cool, quiet, like early morning in a strange house.

I picked out a crayfish and plucked off its claws, then hooked it through the tail and dropped it overboard. White legs wiggled out of sight as line looped off the reel. Just when the bait should have come to rest on the bottom, the line began looping quickly and angled off to deeper water.

I swept back on the rod and a dark, husky smallmouth burst from the water and fell back to the surface with a resounding *whock*!

I glanced around. Perhaps another boat would pull up and see me. But there were no other boats in sight, no one on shore, no one on the island. I would not have minded an audience one bit.

In one of those watching-yourself-while-you're-fishing instances, I looked to slow down and stretch out the situation. To luxuriate in the moment. Downriver, miles away, I could see the wake of a boat on the river's mirrored surface, but not the boat itself. The hedges and groves and barns and houses on Wolfe Island, several miles to the north, stood out like a child's toy farm set.

I felt bigger than life, as the old saying used to go. I was so full of things, full of myself really.

Don was at the dock when I chugged in later that morning. He walked over and eyed my bass.

"You got some fish," he said.

"Yup, in about twenty feet of water off the head of the island." As if he needed to be told.

I thought then, and at several other points that summer, that he might ask me to go fishing with him. As it turned out he never did. He frequently invited my dad to go brant hunting in the fall, but he always fished alone.

I remember quite clearly watching him motor off from the dock in his long duck boat; how he would sit still as a heron in the backseat as he motored out to the bass shoals.

At any rate, I understood that if I wanted to catch bass with any consistency during the summer, I had to get serious about crayfish. My dad helped me seine them from a small creek that flowed through my uncle's dairy farm. That little creek—the headwaters of French Creek where I'd earlier caught chubs on flies—was simply loaded with crayfish and less than 5 miles from Cedar Point. Smallmouth fishing would, that summer, become the purpose of my life.

Later I would realize that using crayfish to catch smallmouth bass did not exactly rank with U-2 flights as a state secret; that anglers everywhere had long used them for bait. For the time being, though, I was an angler in the know, at the top of my game.

CRAYFISH BIOLOGY 101

Numerous scientific studies have confirmed these fishermen's truths, such as they are, and emphasized the often singular importance of crayfish in the smallmouth's diet.

Of particular note is the finding that as smallmouths grow, they consume an increasing biomass of crayfish. A recent study conducted on the New River in West Virginia found that smallmouths begin relying heavily on crayfish during their third year. Studies completed in Alabama, Missouri, Wisconsin, Ohio, Canada, and elsewhere reached similar conclusions, with crayfish comprising 25–90 percent (usually on the upper end) of the total biomass of the diet of adult smallmouths.

There are some 366 species of crayfish in North America, with species diversity greatest in the South. States in the crayfish's southern range may have up to forty species; northern New England states have five or fewer.

Two genera are common in smallmouth habitat. The first, *Orconectes,* originated at the junctions of the Ohio and Missouri Rivers with the Mississippi. From there, different species spread in all directions, as far north as the province of Ontario and as far east as the Atlantic Ocean.

If little crayfish are plentiful on the bottom, bass will ignore every streamer fly or popper in your box.

The second, *Cambarus,* moved from Tennessee northeast along the Appalachians, a sort of high-altitude migration. From there, this genus spread to various watersheds. Today, crayfish of this genus inhabit many of North America's smallmouth waters.

Different species and genera of crayfish may inhabit the same river or lake, but use different microhabitats. Identification probably offers little practical benefit to anglers, however, since anatomical differences remain minimal (*Cambarus* tends to be more heavily "armored," which may make it less desirable in some situations) and coloration, regardless of genus or species, tends to match substrate.

Crayfish frequent a variety of depths. A Lake Michigan *Orconectes* specimen was found, for example, at a depth of 90 feet. For the most part, though, they remain in less than 20 feet of water and spend most of their time on the floor of the lake, pond, or river, moving forward slowly using their smaller walking legs.

When frightened, they shoot backward with a quick downward thrust of their abdomen. Crayfish also avoid predation by waiting for low light before moving about. They become increasingly nocturnal in their second year of life.

Most crayfish have brief life spans, with a few individuals reaching their third summer. They become sexually mature around their first birthday and mate in the spring. Females are said to be in "berry"—that is, pregnant, with fertilized eggs attached to the undersides of their abdomens. Gestation time varies from two to twenty weeks, depending on water temperature.

Crayfish in the same river or lake tend to be on the same biological clock, so the eggs hatch more or less all at once, usually during early summer in smallmouth country. For a few days—the first "instar," in scientific terms—young crayfish venture out for brief periods only to return to the mother's abdomen. They swim off for good once they reach ¾ inch.

Young crayfish grow rapidly in summer light and warm water. Growth occurs through molting (shedding shells). Smaller crayfish, with higher rates of growth, molt most frequently—up to ten times their first year, compared with two or three times during the second year. Crayfish hide in burrows or beneath rocks when they are actually without a shell; however, they tend to be quite active immediately before and after molting. This entire molting period can last five days or more and leaves crayfish quite vulnerable to predation from smallmouth bass.

THE IMPORTANCE OF CRAYFISH SIZE

Although smallmouths remain opportunists when feeding on insects and baitfish, they become quite selective when it comes to crayfish. They prefer smaller specimens and can be very discriminating in their choices.

A study conducted on the New River in West Virginia found smallmouths targeting crayfish in the 1- to 2-inch range. Identifiable crayfish recovered from smallmouths' stomachs were, by the way, 37 percent (total volume) *Orconectes virilis,* 51 percent *Cambarus sciotensis,* and 12 percent *Orconectes sanbornii.*

Another study, this one conducted on streams and rivers in central Ohio, found that bass consistently preferred crayfish 1¼ inches long (*Orconectes sanbornii*) to those 1½ inches long (*Orconectes rusticus*). (This latter species, *rusticus,* also has larger claws and tends to mount a more spirited defense, which may have been a factor in smallmouth selecting *sanbornii.*) Yet another study, this one done on the Current and Jacks Fork Rivers in the Ozarks of south central Missouri, found that smallmouths selected for crayfish (*Orconectes luteus* and *Orconectes punctimanus*) in the 1¼- to 1½-inch range, even though crayfish up to 4 inches long scuttled along the stream bottom.

Most studies have found that smallmouths begin taking crayfish when they reach an inch in length; smaller crayfish remain relatively invulnerable to predation because they can hide quickly in crevices. There is some evidence that, on finer gravel substrate, smallmouths will take smaller crayfish.

Young-of-the-year crayfish in the above studies reached the 1-inch mark in mid-July and early August. Crayfish reach this length at this time, in general, throughout smallmouth range; this explains, in part, why smallmouth "switch" to crayfish in mid- to late summer. A study conducted on Nebish Lake in Wisconsin, for example, found that crayfish (*Orconectes propinquas*) consumption increased from 14.4 percent of food volume in May to 83 percent from July through September.

The same pattern extends throughout the smallmouth's range, in moving water and still. Interestingly enough, while smallmouths' consumption of crayfish increases dramatically during midsummer and early fall, other crayfish-eating fish show no such switch. In the Ozark studies, for instance, rock bass, the chief other predator in the stream, exhibited no seasonal change in prey.

There were other differences, too. Smallmouths in the Ozark study focused on smaller crayfish during the midsummer months, while rock bass moved to crayfish of a larger size. In fact, the biggest smallmouths in the sample appeared the most likely to take crayfish less than 1¼ inches long. This behavior stands in clear contrast with the larger smallmouths' preference for bigger baitfish.

Clearly, small crayfish are a very desirable prey—not only because of their sheer numbers, but for some other reasons as well.

A VULNERABLE PREY

Selectivity can be cut even finer than size. Smallmouths also choose crayfish that look, feel, and behave in certain ways, and these predilections have enormous implications for how we construct and fish our artificials.

As it turns out, when it came to removing a crayfish's claws, Don Wolfe was right, although probably for the wrong reasons. Removing the claws certainly did rule out any crayfish "grabbing the bottom and screwing up your drift," as Don put it. But removing the claws definitely made the crayfish more appealing to small-mouths, too.

A study conducted at the University of Wisconsin (and followed up in the field) found that smallmouths preferred crayfish with smaller, slender claws to those with larger, "lobster" claws. Other recent research has confirmed this pattern. The reason?

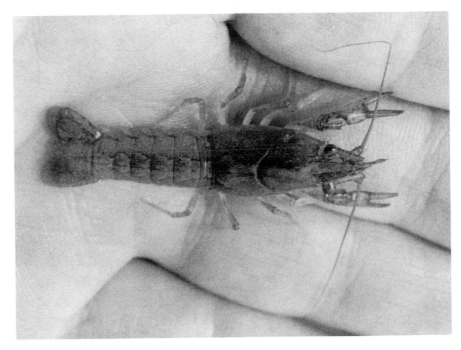

The top of a juvenile crayfish, probably Orconectes. *Note small claws.*

Simple. It's more work for the bass to "handle" (the Wisconsin study's choice of words) the crayfish with larger claws, or "chelae," as they are called.

In fact, when a smallmouth confronted a crayfish with big claws, it often reacted with ambivalence, particularly if the crayfish became aggressive. The bass would flush it, encircle it, and grab it from behind. This maneuvering was quite a bit of work, as the researchers pointed out, and many bass simply turned elsewhere for food. In a sense, the smallmouths found the crayfish "unavailable."

You can imagine this scenario happening across smallmouth range over and over, particularly under cold-front conditions: A sluggish smallmouth bumps up against a big old hardshell; the crayfish waves its claws in defiance; and the bass decides that all the chasing, fighting, and crunching is simply not worth the effort and moves on in search of an easier meal.

By contrast, small claws signify not only vulnerability but the desired juvenile status. The claws on some juveniles can be virtually indistinguishable from the walking legs and barely reach the tip of the nose.

In part, the juveniles' appeal stems from their abundance. But I've always thought there was something more at work, notably that juveniles are much more likely to be softshell than are older, bigger crayfish. Crayfish molt up to ten times their first summer and only two or three times after that. While bass don't have the biological odds down pat, they certainly must know from experience that grabbing a juvenile crayfish could well mean they have a softshell specimen. And if it isn't a softshell? The handling time will likely be minimal because of the small size.

The Wisconsin study did not speak to this issue, but it emphasized the extent to which smallmouths select for molting crayfish. The researchers divided crayfish into five different stages and rank-ordered them from least to most desirable: sexually mature males (males, it should be noted, have bigger chelae than females), berried females, juvenile intermolt (the scientific term for hardshell) males, juvenile intermolt females, and molting crayfish. The study concluded that molting crayfish were by far the most desirable prey, citing the lower percentage of inorganic material (crushed shell, I guess) in a meal of molting crayfish.

You know what? I think smallmouths really like the way softshells taste, too.

Ask any bait fisherman. He'll tell you that smallmouths may ignore hardshells drift after drift, but they'll snatch up a softshell before it touches the bottom.

For what it's worth, I once read a fishing article in a national outdoor magazine that advised anglers to use hardshell crayfish for bait. The author warned that smallmouths would tear the softshells right off the hook. He reminded me of the Vermont storekeeper who refused to stock any more of that new breakfast food because it sold out too fast. Most bait anglers I know learn to put up with bass trying to rip crayfish from their hooks.

Shops along the shores of Lake Ontario and the St. Lawrence River sell crayfish for $1.25 a dozen. Softshells? Three times that much, and many anglers think it no bother at all to keep them in the refrigerator overnight (the cold temperature halts the molting process).

It is this sort of excess, I've been told, that separates normal anglers from true head cases.

That's a quote, by the way.

FLY DESIGN

To be honest, I've always tied crayfish flies to look as much as possible like the kind of softshell crayfish I'd pick out of a bait bucket if I really needed to catch a bass. Small, with softshells and slender chelae—these three qualities make good starting points for any bait or imitation.

Bottom side of a crayfish. Note light coloration.

If you wish to collect some crayfish from a stream bottom rather than a bait tank, make a quick nighttime trip, flashlight in hand, through the shallows of your favorite smallmouth water. A plastic bucket with the bottom removed makes a good one-person crayfish trap. Just plunk it down, reach in, and grab the crayfish. Two people working together can net crayfish rather easily with a minnow seine—day or night. In a pond or lake, haul the seine through the shallows toward shore. In a river, one person can hold the net or screen while the other shuffles along the bottom toward the net. Dislodged crayfish will drift into the mesh.

Try to copy the juveniles in your sample, as it makes sense to keep things small. I use a size 4, 3X long (which produces a fly approximately 1¼ inches long), and tie the imitation with the hook point riding up, which permits me to fish effectively along the bottom.

Crayfish coloration, as noted earlier, reflects the color of the stream or lake substrate. A recently molted crayfish tends to be lighter in color than one with an old carapace, if for no other reason than its shell has yet to scrape on the bottom and develop a layer of dirt and algae. So keep your pattern on the light side. Tints of cream, light olive, light gray, light brown, and buff make good general colors.

Author's softshelled crayfish fly, top view.

The claws or chelae have, over the years, come to represent the defining feature of nearly every traditional crayfish imitation. These pincers, typically bunches of bucktail, often end up bigger than the crayfish itself and traditionally flare out the end of the body at the bend of the hook. Examinations of actual crayfish, however, show that the chelae join the body at the midpoint of the cephalothorax, not at the nose.

More to the point, smallmouths clearly select for crayfish with the smallest chelae or claws. The irony is remarkable: The very feature that dominates fly patterns, indeed identifies a crayfish pattern as such, may actually cue smallmouths to look elsewhere for a meal!

So keep your chelae wispy. Fibers from partridge hackles make good claws, as do sparse pinches of soft hairs from furs such as lynx and fox. Whatever the material, the chelae should not extend much beyond the nose of the fly.

Given the way smallmouths select for softshelled crayfish, texture may be the most important consideration of all. Smallmouths will mouth a real crayfish to determine the hardness of the shell, and I've watched and felt them nip at a fly.

A single layer of bucktail makes a good carapace. It should be slightly darker than the roughly dubbed and picked-out underbody of fox fur and Antron. This arrangement gives the feel and appearance of a molting crayfish: a thin, medium-toned outer shell with light-colored, soft flesh inside.

The use of soft materials—grouse feathers and fox fur and Antron—is the key to suggesting a molting crayfish. Whether you tie, buy, or both, virtually any pattern can

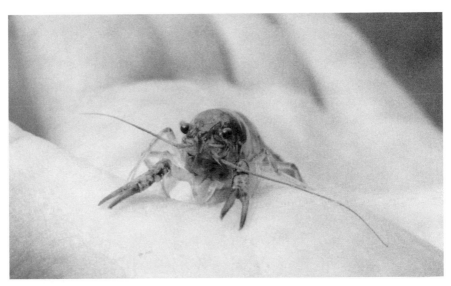

Front view of crayfish.

be improved by picking out the fur and thinning and trimming the claws. The more chewed up a crayfish pattern gets the better it works. Some of my best flies have been so mauled and pecked at by fish that the bucktail has been virtually chewed away. I've tried all-fur patterns without the bucktail carapace, by the way, and they just don't work as well. (See appendix C for tying instructions.)

This particular pattern owes a debt to other imitations, of course. Like any flies, crayfish patterns have evolved over the years, although only recently have tyers shown much interest in imitating the softshell phase.

A number of fine imitations have appeared in the last decade, including Whitlock's Softshell Crayfish, Crawfish Impersonator, Crawdad Shedder, Ted's Crayfish, Joe Robinson's Mud Bug, and the Clouser Crayfish, to name a few. New patterns often emphasize the softshell phase in the choice of materials and imitative features.

There are many ways to suggest a molting crayfish, of course, and exciting, effective new imitations appear every year. In response to a recent magazine article, three different anglers included their softshell crayfish "ties" in letters they sent me. The most effective patterns clearly are in our future.

In the end, the idea of constructing a pattern to imitate vulnerable prey is nothing new; after all, streamers suggest a crippled or disoriented minnow, spinner patterns certainly imitate mayflies at their most vulnerable state, and emergers, stillborns, and so forth all work on a similar principle.

Crayfish patterns are just catching up with the rest of the fly-fishing world, that's all.

Front view of author's softshelled crayfish fly.

FISHING CRAYFISH FLIES

As described in chapter 9, prey behavior has a significant influence on smallmouth predation. So it is that crayfish behavior can at times determine whether a bass strikes. The idea behind presentation is the same as that behind design: vulnerability. It draws greatly upon the "available" part of the overall abundant-and-available rule that dictates smallmouth feeding behavior.

Recall, for instance, the Wisconsin study, in which smallmouths didn't like to chase their crayfish. "Handling time" remained a key variable in determining whether bass actually took the crayfish. Make it easy for them.

In flowing water, long gravel riffles often have uniform currents that accommodate sink-tip lines and a cross-stream presentation. Here's how: Cast across and upstream, and mend the line to get the fly near the bottom (this is important). Let the crayfish fly drift, trying to minimize drag all the while. Then let the fly swing around. When it does, feed a little line so that the fly comes to rest on the bottom of the pool, hopefully in some slack water just off the current. Hand-twist the fly back along the gravel and rubble.

The upstream dead-drift presentation is probably useful in more streamside situations. It lets you fish the slots between boulders and the deep transitional runs that bigger bass often favor. The upstream drift works well in current seams and eddies near the heads of pools, too.

The presentation is the same as with upstream nymphing, and so is the best rig: a floating line, a 7½- to 9-foot leader, and whatever split shot you need to keep the crayfish pattern dribbling along the bottom.

As with nymphing, strikes are often barely detectable. Other times they may come as a light *tick* or steady pressure, not unlike the take of a bass as it picks up a live crayfish. Sometimes you'll feel the fish nipping at the fly before taking it. Set the hook forcefully by yanking down with the loose line while lifting swiftly and simultaneously with the rod.

Detecting strikes in still water is much the same; otherwise, fishing these imitations in lakes and ponds differs considerably from fishing them in rivers and streams.

Everything is deeper, for one thing, usually in the 10- to 20-foot range. Rubble or gravel bottom interspersed with boulder and rock is usually a good place to fish a crayfish imitation.

The depths require a longer, faster sink-tip line or a full-sink line and a 2- to 3-foot leader. If you need split shot, add it to the butt of the leader near the line so you can pull free from the rocks.

The trick is to retrieve the fly inch by inch, with a hand-twist. For whatever reason, I have far more patience with subsurface imitations than with bass bugs. My metabolism just plain slows down whenever I tie on a crayfish imitation; maybe it's the bait fisherman in me.

At any rate, I've always been amazed by how slowly you must retrieve a fly to make it actually "crawl" across the bottom. If you've never done it, try this experiment. Wade into knee-deep water, drop the crayfish pattern so that it comes to rest on the bottom, and shake out some line from your rod. Bend down close to the surface, so that you can watch your fly, and begin hand-twisting the line. Check out how slowly the hand-twist must proceed in order to make the crayfish pattern actually creep across the lake floor. You can also see how much line you need to strip to make the crayfish pattern scoot a couple feet, as if to escape.

The hand-twist and the scoot are the two most important still-water crayfish retrieves. After scooting the fly, let it rest right on bottom, the way a real crayfish might after escaping a predator. I often leave the crayfish pattern motionless for a minute or two at a time, particularly if the fish seem inactive. Sometimes, in fact, you can't retrieve your fly slowly enough.

I remember one such evening, fishing on a shoal near Henderson Harbor on Lake Ontario with my friend Lee Ellsworth. I was midway through a bottom-crawling retrieve when Lee hooked a bass on a live crayfish. He played it to the boat, and I laid down my fly rod and picked up my camera to take a picture of him landing and releasing the fish.

Lee looked past me even as he was landing the smallmouth.

"Hey, look at your rod tip," he said. "You've got a bite. Looks like a bullhead."

It did look like a bullhead bite—several gentle twitches, then a stronger pull. I reached back, picked up the rod, and, standing and gathering the slack, set the hook into a good smallmouth—nearly 15 inches, it turned out.

Some twenty minutes later, Lee once again landed a good-sized bass—the fish were coming quickly that evening—and once again I began clicking pictures.

"You're not gonna believe this," Lee said. "But you've got another bite on your fly rod."

I was in the middle of composing the picture; the light was perfect. "I'll get it in a second."

"You better get it right now!" he said in a rising voice. I turned and snared the rod as it clattered along the gunnel. I grabbed it just above the butt, and the graphite rod buckled with a crunch, right in my hand.

This remains the one time in my life that a fish actually broke my fly rod. I've ruined my share of rods in my day, but all the others met with a boot, door, or tailgate. Two years ago I even drove off with my fly rod on top of my car. But this rod gave way to an honest-to-goodness fish.

The bass itself was a 12-incher, maybe 13, certainly not the size you would expect of a rod-breaker. It had all happened so fast. I grabbed line and rod together in my fist, and with the deep water and aggressive fish the pressure was more than the rod could bear.

For the remainder of the evening, I fixed my fly reel to one of Lee's spinning rods and came to appreciate the facility of the modern fly-rod system.

Still, I kept on hooking smallmouths. They were biting; fly or bait, it didn't matter. We were at the end of a period of high pressure, and dusk developed gradually beneath a pastel-streaked evening sky that stretched out across Lake Ontario to the Canadian lake plain. The bass had been on that particular shoal for a few days, gorging on crayfish (Lee also caught them on minnows, jigs, and crawlers), and they had no reason at all to leave or even to modify their piggish behavior.

Across the continent, lakes, ponds, and rivers hum with life and streamside twilights linger long. Smallmouth waters have a special fecundity about them in August, and fishing crayfish patterns along the bottom puts the fly fisher in the right place at the right time.

These are smallmouths at their best, fat and healthy, hooked beneath a summer sky. At the bite of the hook, they often shoot straight from the bottom to the surface. It's one of those definitive moments in fishing. You can see the bright fly line lift through the water, and you wait, as time stops, for the bass to leap clear of the water and the scene to complete itself—and what a delicious, suspenseful instant: How big will this fish be? And there it is. Twisting, head shaking in a blur, bigger than you thought.

Many anglers are pleasantly surprised when they hook their first smallmouth on a crayfish pattern. Much of the glamour of smallmouth fishing has been connected with the surface: The closer to the surface, the more exciting the fishing. We often extend this idea to bottom-fishing, with a corollary that the closer to the bottom, the duller the fishing.

Taking a few bass on crayfish imitations usually changes that presumption.

11

Finding Smallmouths in Lakes, Reservoirs, and Major Rivers

By the turn of the century, fishing for smallmouth bass was well established in major lakes and rivers across the land. It's just that nobody caught them on flies. Live bait—"minnies" and crayfish—was the usual choice of guides working these big waters.

The dichotomy continues today, although increasing numbers of fly fishers are focusing their efforts on larger waters. Still, most experienced fly fishers who get the smallmouth bug pull on their waders and head for streams and other places where smallmouths behave like trout. Most of those fly fishing the larger waters do so during June and early July, when bass are in shallow water. After that, the big waters see few fly fishers; the Great Lakes and major reservoirs and lakes around the country remain the province of bass boats, tournaments, guides, and live bait.

Big waters create their own environment. A river may run through it, but with Lake Michigan, for example, you could only say that the land extends around it. True, the former may hold the essence of the fishing life—but the latter expresses the enormity of it.

In 1980, the Thousand Islands region of eastern Lake Ontario and the St. Lawrence finally hosted a national bass fishing tournament, and a number of the pros exclaimed to the press that they'd never seen so many bass—smallmouths and largemouths—anywhere in the country.

The next day, a number of them went out and flipped their bass boats trying to negotiate heavy seas and 40-mile-per-hour winds.

For our purposes, an open lake is certainly not the easiest place to fish with a fly rod. But it sure is an interesting one.

SMALLMOUTH LOCATION

In a stream or pond, catching smallmouths begins and ends with presenting the right fly or using the right strategy. You know basically where the fish are. In the big waters, by contrast, their location is never a given.

As noted earlier, smallmouths tend to be homebodies, although they occupy different home ranges of different sizes at various times of the year. Wintering and spawning areas are each quite limited. Their summer home range is a different matter.

In extensive studies conducted in Algonquin Park, Ontario, Mark Ridgway found the home range for summer smallmouths to average 400–600 acres. The fish made use of the entire range every day, nearly always swimming in schools, and covering up to 7 miles daily around and around the entire home range on their "trapline," as Ridgway called it. The smallmouths in this study area relied extensively on crayfish, and that, Ridgway speculated, is what forced them to remain on the move.

Research has also indicated (see chapter 3) that, given the complexity of the largest bodies of water, there are no doubt a number of distinct populations of bass in the same lake or same area of a larger lake. These populations frequent different habitats and even take different forage.

For anglers this means that smallmouths' preferred locations change as the summer deepens and as forage locations shift. Which is why, when big-water bass fishing gets tough, people talk about "finding" them, not "fooling" them.

On big waters like the Great Lakes or St. Lawrence, the patterns of summer smallmouths tend to shift through the season in the same way every year. This is how Don Wolfe, an experienced angler who had fished the river for so many years, always knew where the bass were, or at least where they should be. And all the other fishermen knew that he knew. You could tell how tough the fishing was by how many boats were following him out of harbor.

I can remember standing by the marina at Cedar Point with my father one day.

"Come here," Fran Garrett, the park superintendent, said to us. "Look at this."

We walked up to where he stood on a hill in back of the marina. We could see out over the river, see Don motoring out toward his secret spot on Middle Shoal, behind him a trail of three or four other boats.

"Like a goddamn mother duck and her ducklings," Fran laughed. It was a good image—I still remember it thirty-five years later—though Don didn't exactly evoke motherhood in his demeanor. Rumor had it, in fact, that he kept his 10-gauge brant gun on board, which might explain why the other boats remained several hundred yards behind.

Nevertheless they followed him, a recognition of the reality of open-water small-mouth fishing. As Don used to say, "There's a lot more places where they aren't than where they are."

One night after dark I walked down to the dock. Don was sitting in his boat, smoking, drinking a beer.

A marina at night feels strange, like a stadium without fans. No racing engines or squealing kids. No knots of tourists. No wash from boat wakes. Just flat, black water. An occasional rope creaking on a dock cleat.

Don had just come in from fishing, it appeared. And he had his usual catch of bass. Good ones. I could hear the chain stringer clanking on the side of his boat.

"Middle Shoal?"

"Nope, Linda Island."

That's where I'd been fishing for the last two days. Hard. One keeper bass to my name. "I tried it there today, too," I said, sitting down on the edge of the dock next to the bow of his boat. I didn't know what to say. It was my fifth summer fishing here. I was thirteen, beyond "Gee, how'd you catch 'em, mister?"

Panfish smacked at the surface out in the blackness. Voices echoed from the concession stand back by the beach. You could hear the jukebox. The snack bar was kept open at night, mostly to keep the teenagers centralized, I suppose, which made it easier to keep an eye on them. Some of them were friends, but it was mostly an older crowd. Bass fishing wasn't a hot topic.

"Those bass were really bunched up, right on a ledge at the head of the island. Never seen them up that high this early. They're usually not there until August," Don said. "It took me all night to find them."

I hadn't tried it there. "That's pretty high up," I said, following the tune, squinting back at Don in the yellow docklight.

"You're goddamn right it is."

"Were you as far up as the point of the island?"

"Beyond that," Don said, taking a deep drag on his cigarette. "You've got to line up the boulder at the head of the island with the red boathouse in Sand Bay."

"Yeah, I know where you mean."

"That will give you the mark for how far up along the island you should be. Next, look downriver and line up the lighthouse just out from the foot of the island with the cluster of three islands on the horizon down by Clayton. That will give you the distance out from the island.

"You've got to get upriver from the first mark before you drop your anchor." Don flipped his cigarette out into the darkness, and it hit the water with a sharp hiss.

"Well, it was a little slow where I was fishing down lower. Maybe I'll try it up there, if you don't mind," I said, getting up to go.

"I don't mind at all."

The next morning dawned warm and still. The smells of the river clinging to the harbor. I headed out in a cloud of blue smoke from my prewar outboard (a '39 Sears that still runs, by the way).

Rock pile and red roof, lighthouse and cluster of islands; rock pile and red roof, lighthouse and islands.

In retrospect it was not a question of "Could I remember?" It was more "Could I ever forget?"

Some eight hours later I pulled up the anchor and returned to the dock. Time to call it a day; time for dinner. I wrapped the cord around the knuckle-buster spin wheel on the outboard. With a yank, it coughed and sputtered to life.

I had five keeper bass on my stringer, two of them 15 inches, one an 18-incher. Three pounds easy. I hoisted them into the boat and chugged home, hungry, smelling the wood smoke drifting out across the water from the state park campfires.

Then I saw Don approaching in his boat, just leaving the marina, heading out to fish for the evening. When we passed, I waved and he waved back.

Us river men shared an unspoken bond.

SUMMER STRUCTURES

A number of morals can be drawn from this story, and one of them is that, properly placed with the right bait, just about anybody can catch smallmouth bass in late summer.

If there is a key to locating them, it's identifying transitions in the composition of the bottom. Smaller lakes and bigger rivers may have bottoms of mud, silt, and sand. In those instances, finding bass means finding rocky bottom—rubble or gravel.

In lakes or sections of big lakes, an isolated stretch of rocky bottom in a larger area of weeds, sand, or mud can also produce bass. The reverse is true, too: Find the only weed bed in a vast area of stone and you'll likely find fish. Rocks and rubble mean

Ultimately a fish of transition, smallmouths will gravitate to a patch of gravel surrounded by weeds, as well as to a copse of weeds in an area of gravel. Both structures offer good foraging for baitfish.

crayfish, sculpins, and darters; weeds spell soft-finned baitfish. These microstructures—and those that follow—are stops on the smallmouth's "trapline."

Deep weedlines can be a good area for baitfish—smallmouths, too, but this is more *Esox* territory, northerns in particular. A line of boulders extending out from a point into deep water makes better smallmouth structure. The rocks attract both baitfish and crayfish. Reservoirs, in particular, sometimes have old stone walls and roadways that run into the water and provide excellent smallmouth habitat. You may be able to identify these structures by scanning the surrounding hillsides or looking at old topo maps.

Things get more complicated with the largest lakes and rivers, if only because the shoreline offers few clues as to what's beneath the surface. But near these bigger wa-

An old stone wall running into a reservoir often holds plentiful smallmouth forage, namely crayfish and baitfish.

ters are bait stores, which dispense advice and sell depth charts and fishing charts. Each of these—probably in that order—is useful for locating fish your first time on the water.

Bottom composition remains the most significant component in locating a fishing spot. Look for a mix—rubble, gravel, and boulder, with an occasional weed tuft here and there. You can find these spots along the shoreline, most frequently in the form of a shelf that extends quite a way out into deep water. While the boulder and weed tufts are nice, it's the gravel and rubble that crayfish need, and this is the kind of bottom bass can catch them on. Find it in 10–25 feet of water, and active summer smallmouths almost certainly will be frequent visitors.

Most big-water anglers look to offshore shoals, the classic structures. Best depths? Anything that "shoals" to 5–30 feet from surrounding depths of 20–100 feet, respectively. Summer smallmouths generally remain in the 10–40-foot range. All things being

An offshore shoal is the classic big-water smallmouth spot. The best ones include a diversity of habitat such as boulders, gravel, and weed tufts.

equal, smallmouths often swim in water that is 18–20 degrees Celsius or in the mid-60s Fahrenheit. So I suppose 15 feet of water makes a good starting point. If the water has a bit of a stain to it, start on the shallow side; if it's very clear, go to the deeper side. (Dawn and dusk and windy conditions may find fish in shallower water, too.)

In the last few years, the water of the Great Lakes has become remarkably clear because of the influx of zebra mussels, which are filter feeders. It's possible to see bottom in up to 40–50 feet of water. The effect on the smallmouths, at this point, is unclear. On Lake Ontario, anglers are having luck fishing in deeper water of 25–30 feet—and more. On Lake Michigan, however, anglers continue to have good luck in depths of under 12 feet, according to Chicago angler and writer Bob Long Jr. The difference may have to do with water temperature. Michigan's surface seldom gets above the mid-60s; Lake Ontario, on the other hand, commonly approaches the upper 70s. But at this point no one knows for sure.

Depth finders can be very useful for locating shoals on big lakes.

Electronic depth finders can be very useful in finding productive areas. Depth charts can identify prime locations, too, if not with quite the same precision. When I was drift-fishing at Cedar Point, I'd throw over a decoy anchor on 15 feet of cord; whenever I heard it clank on rock I'd anchor and fish. Today's anglers usually spring for the digital models.

Like most smallmouth anglers, I get excited about shoals with highly pronounced depth changes, but I can point to little evidence that such a characteristic really means a better place to bass fish. Indeed, rock piles that zoom out of deep water can provide exceptional fishing, but they can't withstand heavy foraging from bass. The fishing can be hit or miss.

An ideal shoreline or island shoal, with grassy drop-offs, gravel/boulder shelf, and deep drop-off.

What really determines the productivity of a shoal is its surface area. Larger shoals simply produce a lot of smallmouth forage, which results in many return customers. The shoal near Cedar Point is a good example; it continues to produce bass today.

Structurally, it's not a true offshore shoal, but a shelf that extends from an island into the river channel. The depth varies from 10 to 30 feet before falling to 60 and then 100 feet or more in the river channel. The shelf or shoal represents a considerable depth change from the surrounding bottom, and the shoal itself has a number of humps and holes. Crayfish, minnows, and fry proliferate; no doubt some of the humps and holes have more forage than others.

I say this because some of the spots on the shoal are much better than others, and the one Don Wolfe had me set up on, I later came to realize, was a gravel and rubble hump some 30–50 yards in area. At the head is a small ledge, which is what the anchor catches on. I was fishing on a spot that was 15 feet deep, surrounded by boulders and weeds on one side toward the island and 35 feet of water on the other three.

You often hear how smallmouths go to deep water during the summer. Sometimes they do, but not always, by any stretch. A shallow (3- to 10-foot) gravel pocket or rock hump surrounded by weeds can provide excellent and overlooked fishing. Smallmouths move into these areas in search of shiners, minnows, and fry, even during some of the warmest days of late summer.

If the shallow-water gravel patch represents an overlooked spot, the sharp shoreline drop-off probably represents one that is overfished. Cliffs and steep drop-offs always look like they should have plenty of bass. Often they do, if—and this is a big if—the bottom composition will hold forage.

The sheer granite walls that look so sexy are actually inferior—at least from an angler's viewpoint—to those cliffs with checkerboard faces. The more that wind and water have chipped away at the stone, the more that rocks and boulders have fallen into the water, the more habitat there will be for baitfish and crayfish.

A final spot not to be overlooked is the creek channel or "hole"—particularly in a shallow lake. Sometimes fish will hold on the edge of the drop-off (it doesn't have to be a dramatic depth change; those that go from, say, 8 to 12 feet are often the best); other times they will be on the bottom of the channel. If the channel bottom offers a different composition and a current, too, you just may have a spot worth remembering. Fish the channel where it bends and provides a current break.

Smallmouth structures, in short, involve anything that attracts forage or represents some sort of transition. Bottom composition, surface area, depth change, and current pressure are all important considerations, and their importance is roughly in that order.

HEAT AND HIGH PRESSURE

A little heat is usually good for smallmouth fishing in northern areas. But it can get too hot. Back in the early 1970s, while spending the summer on Shelburne Point on Lake Champlain in Vermont, I encountered some seriously hot weather.

For at least two weeks it had been blistering hot. Gorgeous gravel shoals and points and islands produced nothing but bug-eyed rock bass, the five-inch kind that are three-quarters mouth and the rest tail. Early morning, I realized with more than a little trepidation, presented the best opportunity to catch some bass.

The world at 5 A.M. is a weird place if you're not used to it. But here I was, risking dangerous REM deprivation and motoring out to a gravel shoal. I'd dragged along my girlfriend, Buffy, so that I wouldn't fall asleep at the tiller.

Reaching the shoal that stretched between two moored sailboats, I cast out a live crayfish on my ultralight spinning rod—this was before I did any fly fishing for smallmouths—and hooked a fish as the boat glided to a halt.

It blew out of the water immediately, and it was big, really big—four pounds easy. It ran past the bow, away from the boat. With two-pound-test line, there was no stopping it.

I climbed up in the bow while Buffy took my seat in the stern. Again the bass jumped, a truly magnificent fish. It zoomed back beneath the boat, and I reeled madly to keep up with it.

"Grab an oar and paddle on the left so we can turn the bow," I said. Buffy did, but the bass had turned, and now I was playing the fish over my shoulder. "Other side!"

"I get it. I'll paddle on the other. . . ." And I felt a solid crack on the back of my head. Everything got cottony and sparkly, and from miles away I heard words: "God, I hit you with the oar. Are you O.K.?"

"Uh, yeah, I'm O.K. I'm O.K." My own words sounded strange, too, like they were coming at me, not from me.

Well, here I was, right here, holding on to a fishing rod. With a big, goddamn bass flopping around on my line.

As it turned out, I landed the fish, an ounce short of 4 pounds. Better yet, I didn't need stitches. And in the days to come we got the early-morning thing in better sync (shorter oars!).

And every morning we'd go out, and it would be cool and still, and the smallmouths would bite—until the sun hit the water and the heat wave kicked into gear.

That month on Champlain certainly convinced me of the power of first light during hot weather, but it also gave me cause to rethink one of the canons of smallmouth lore: during midsummer, the fish in any given body of water hold at one depth only, and to catch them you must fish at *that* depth. Those Lake Champlain smallmouths held at depths between 5 and 25 feet. When they bit at one spot, they bit at the other. And when they stopped—which they did every day at 9 A.M. or so—they stopped biting everywhere—even in the deep water just over the edge of the drop-off. All I ever caught after 9 A.M. were rock bass. And you couldn't stand the heat anyway.

From what I know now, I think those Champlain smallmouths left the area entirely once they appeared to "stop biting." Having moved on to these spots far inside Shelburne Bay before first light, they must have moved on again around 9 A.M., continuing on the deep-water leg of their "trapline." That particular stretch could have been a mile or more from the relatively shallow waters of the interior bay. No one knows for sure, of course. But what else explains the lights-out phenomenon inside the bay—even where the depth reached 30 feet and more?

Last summer I returned to Lake Champlain to fish the deep-water bluffs around Shelburne and Thompson's Points. I'd fished the waters at the southern and northern ends of the lake quite a bit in recent times, but I hadn't fished back here in more than twenty years.

I fished with my friends Tom Fuller, Marcel Rocheleau, and Shawn Gregoire, out of Shawn's boat. Tom and I reached Shawn's South Burlington apartment after dark. Inside, Marcel and Shawn were drinking beer and tying streamers.

They both regaled us with the excellent fishing. "It's great," Marcie explained. "We use the electric trolling motor, ease along the drop-offs, and the bass bounce right up from the bottom."

"How deep?" Tom asked.

"Well, probably in eight to ten feet of water, but it's right on a drop-off that falls to thirty feet or more. The fish come right up to take the streamer. White's been the best color. They're feeding on minnows, I think."

"We got to get there early," Shawn added. "On the water by five-thirty. The fishing's pretty much over by nine. I think the bass go back to deep water."

Outside came the sound of rain rattling on the window. Thunder rumbled in the distance. I couldn't believe it. "Hey, I thought the weather was supposed to be good for tomorrow?"

"Supposed to be good until Sunday morning," Shawn said, jabbing the changer at the TV. On the Weather Channel, the forecast. Tonight: Rain, heavy at times. Dangerous lightning. Clearing toward morning. Saturday: Partly cloudy, much cooler. Highs in the low 60s. Winds from the northwest at 5–10 miles per hour, increasing to 10–20 by midday.

"Shit, I thought the front was supposed to hold off another day," Shawn said. "This afternoon they were calling for partly cloudy and warm. We're screwed."

Tom, Marcel, and I avoided the temptation to add any false optimism. We knew better.

And the next morning, the weather was clear and bright and cool. At first it wasn't that windy, and Shawn managed to keep us in the lee when the wind came up later in the morning.

But it didn't matter. We finished until noon in the clear green water, with the tops of boulders visible 15 feet down. High crumbling cliffs towered above us when we edged in to fish tight to the drop-offs. The Adirondacks rose to the west, the Green Mountains to the east. It was great to be back.

We never boated a bass.

PLATE 1: *Floaters and Swimmers*

1. Tap's Bug
2. Sneaky Pete
3. Dahlberg Diver
4. Whitlock's Damsel
5. Messinger Bucktail Frog
6. Swimming Frog
7. Most Whit Hair Bug
8. White Fly

Please see Appendix C for details on these fly patterns and the three plates following.

PLATE 2: Streamers

9.   Clouser Ultra Deep Minnow
10. Marabou Shiner
11. Marabou Thunder Creek

12. Marabou Matuka
13. Sculpin/Darter Marabou Muddler
14. Woolly-headed Sculpin

PLATE 3: Nymphs

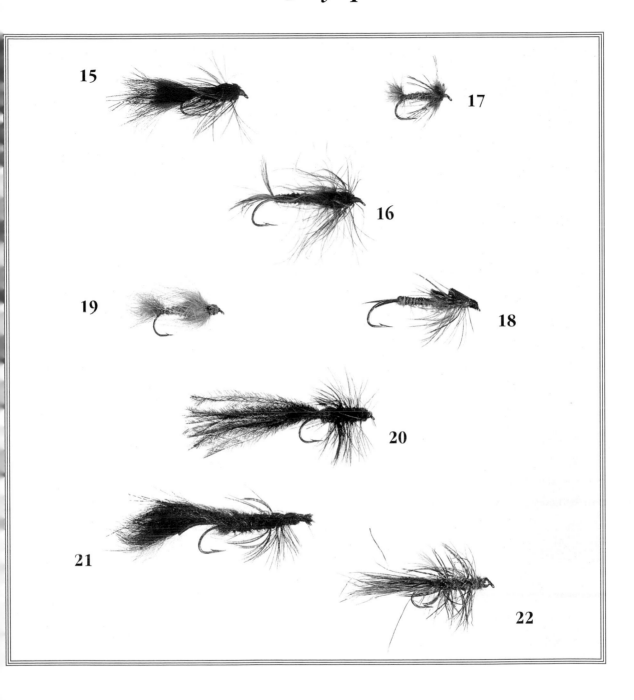

15. Clouser Swimming Nymph
16. Brooks' Stone
17. The Sparrow
18. Turkey Feather Stonefly Nymph
19. Art's Casual Dress
20. Murray's Hellgrammite
21. Furry Hellgrammite
22. Bead-head March Brown Bugger

PLATE 4: *Crayfish, Grubs, and Leeches*

23. Schley's Crayfish
24. Clouser Crayfish
25. Softshell Crayfish

26. BossBob's Dubbed Crayfish
27. BossBob's Leech
28. Sparkle Grub

12 Open-Water Patterns and Presentations

G uides on lakes, reservoirs, and big rivers like fishing for smallmouth bass. They know where to find them, and once they get out to the spot their clients generally have little trouble catching them. Even Aunt Edna, who hasn't been fishing since Eisenhower was president, can put a few in the livewell with live shiners or crayfish.

Fly rodders usually have a tougher time fishing the big water, which is part of the reason, I suppose, that so few do it.

Some years ago, my fishing friends Steve Boyer and John Kaufman came to visit for a weekend of smallmouth fishing in the Thousand Islands. They arrived on Friday evening, and I could see they wanted to dispense with amenities and get fishing. They acted antsy, lots of one-word responses to my questions about how they'd been since I'd seen them last: "Good." "Fine." "Yup." Like that.

John planned on using marabou streamers, but Steve had purchased a bucket of shiners from the Chaumont Bay bait shop. Owner Larry Comins nets his minnows from the very shore we'd be fishing. A weather front was moving in. It was as close as smallmouth fishing gets to a lock.

They were pumped.

"Go ahead," I said. "I've been fishing all week. I want to stay and clean up a. . . ." I finished my sentence to a banging screen door.

It was a calm evening with high cloud cover, and from the cottage deck I watched them head out across the broad bay in a 13-foot outboard toward a small knot of boats clustered off a distant point. The bass had been there every day, feeding on the vast schools of lake minnows that lived in the weed beds in these shallow bays. The point was at the head of Hardscrabble Bay, one of the richest smallmouth areas on eastern Lake Ontario.

They returned after dark, and I walked down to the dock to see how they'd made out. They had four good ones, just right for dinner. John shone the flashlight while Steve did the filleting.

"How'd the streamers work?" I asked John.

"Good," John said. "Not as good as shiners, but good. I'd pick up a bass on every drift; Steve would get two to my every one."

In the fifteen years or so since that evening, I've seen nothing that would cause me to modify John's assessment of the relative effectiveness of flies and bait. When it comes to big-water fishing during the summer, a good fly fisher (and Kaufman is a very good fly fisher) can stay with a bait angler, particularly during the first half hour or so of working a school. Over the course of the day, a fly fisher will catch one bass to every two for an angler fishing with bait. If the water approaches 20 feet, make that one to every three. A good jig fisher falls somewhere in between—catching more than those using flies, fewer than those using bait. Not always, of course. But most of the time.

It's not unusual for a fly, particularly a crayfish imitation, to do better than bait initially. Perhaps the fly drifts in full view of the school, whereas baits and sinkers often hide or settle into the crevices of rocks.

IMITATING OPEN-WATER FORAGE

The best open-water smallmouth patterns usually imitate either baitfish or crayfish. Marabou streamers make top choices, as do Clouser Minnows. Crayfish patterns may well be as important as streamers. Lightly fished smallmouths often take any crayfish fly; those that get fished a lot expect something a bit more appealing.

After those top-shelf imitations come some other good selections. The Muddler Minnow (with a mottled turkey wing) makes a good general bottom imitation, as it does a decent job with sculpins and crayfish. Woolly Buggers, in purple, black, white, tan, yellow, chartreuse, and mottled olive-brown, often prove effective sculpin/darter imitations. Other soft-hackled patterns may come in handy, too. The Sparrow is my favorite, but the Casual Dress is a good choice as well.

O.K., so all these flies catch fish. They really do. But, as John Kaufman noted years ago, it's tough to keep up with the bait- and spin fishers—particularly those who can handle jigs. And day in, day out, under various conditions, depths, and presentations,

Day in, day out, no artificials come close to matching the effectiveness of tube jigs like this Mister Twister.

few artificials of any kind can match the overall effectiveness of plastic-tube jigs. Indeed, no artificial has had a comparable effect on smallmouth fishing in the last twenty years. From the dusty shelves of ramshackle marinas to the glittering booths at sporting shows, these bright-colored slivers of plastic dominate the smallmouth bass fishing world. Mister Twisters, Gitsits, Power Grubs, and all the rest are the lures of choice for professional bass fishers. They work for smallmouths in all sorts of habitat, particularly in open water, and it is not at all irrelevant to explore why.

The three-year study conducted on New York's Canadarago Lake back in the late 1970s, noted in chapter 9, sheds some interesting light on this question. Recall that researchers found that yellow perch comprised approximately 75 percent of the smallmouths' diet, a reflection of the lake's huge populations of perch fry. Tessellated darters were next in preference, representing approximately 12 percent of the smallmouth's diet. Crayfish comprised less than 3 percent. (Actually, this number is bit shaky. Crayfish tended to show up in the stomachs of angler-caught bass, meaning some of them may have ended up in the smallmouths' stomachs courtesy of slow-striking bait fishers.)

Given the extent to which perch dominate the smallmouth's diet, you'd think that spin fishers would clean up with a perch-patterned Rapala or crankbait, or perhaps a yellow spinner.

Well, forget it. The best lures? According to a magazine article written on the lake several years after the study, the most effective artificials were black and purple Mister Twisters. Live crayfish were popular with bait fishers.

I phoned the article's author, Bob McNitt, friend and editor of *New York Sportsman,* to find out why perch-patterned crankbaits or Rapalas weren't included in the list of best lures.

"To tell the truth, you never heard much about them," McNitt explained. "Though if you were going to use them anywhere, this would be the place. The lake's loaded with little perch."

There it is. For many trout anglers, this scenario gets to the heart of their indifference toward smallmouths: Determining the forage does not lead to determining the right fly pattern. Trout fishing's venerable presumption, by contrast, is that you need to figure out "what they're taking." That you then need to imitate what the trout are eating seems so obvious, stating it borders on the banal.

This trout-think works for smallmouth fishing, too, most typically in streams. It also applies to open water when smallmouths have keyed into big numbers of a preferred forage, such as crayfish, emerald shiners, spot-tailed minnows, or alewives.

But at other times smallmouths end up taking what they can get—and keep an eye out for something better. Like the smallmouths on Canadarago.

Selective opportunism, in other words. Or, the idea of preferred forage versus consumed forage, a concept that emerged in the New River study (see chapter 7) in which hellgrammites were unavailable as forage, but highly desired nevertheless. In the Canadarago study, darters were more important to smallmouths than to pickerel and largemouths; perch, by contrast, were not. Crayfish were popular far out of proportion to the frequency of their occurrence in stomach samples. Clearly, these two prey species were the smallmouth's preferred forage.

But Mister Twisters? Why them? Well, start with their tubular profile. Their shape certainly suggests darters and crayfish. And there's more. As Mark Ridgway's underwater observations in Algonquin Park indicate, smallmouths seem to be "taken" by the action of Mister Twister. The soft texture and wriggling tail of the plastic bait evoke images of molting crayfish, perhaps, or the large fins of a darter hovering over the bottom. With a hopping/jigging retrieve along the bottom and its lifelike texture and movement, a Mister Twister makes all the right moves in all the right places.

For the record, the tubular shape, rubbery texture, and location on the bottom also call to mind the hellgrammite. All the more reason, I guess, that these soft, plastic, tube-shaped lures work across smallmouth range, in all water types, and at all times of the year.

Naturally, were I going to fish a lake with the perch fry that Canadarago has, I'd tie up some yellow and olive marabou streamers. Half the fun of fly fishing is developing and fishing an imitation of what the smallmouths are eating. I'm just no longer that surprised when it doesn't work.

And Mister Twisters or any other plastic-tube jigs do.

REVENGE OF THE TWISTER FLY

Anglers often use imitative plastic forms like shad, minnow, and crayfish shapes (and colors). But they also use them with little thought about what they imitate—as the popularity of black and purple Mister Twisters on Canadarago Lake suggests. Motor oil, pumpkinseed, red, blue, purple, pearl, smoke, white, yellow, bubble gum, hot orange, and, above all, chartreuse are all quite popular—depending on weather, water stain, and forage choices. And probably astro charts, too.

At any rate, over the years fishing friends have caught bass after bass on these weird-looking globs of plastic. And to tell you the truth, I'd gotten pretty sick of it. So

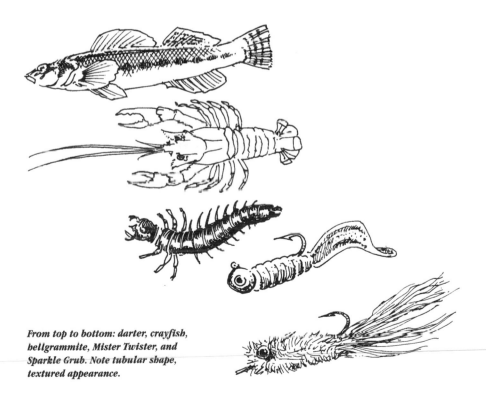

From top to bottom: darter, crayfish, hellgrammite, Mister Twister, and Sparkle Grub. Note tubular shape, textured appearance.

This midday summer bass took a Sparkle Grub fished in a gravel patch surrounded by weeds.

several years ago I forgot all about imitating naturals and worked on designing a fly that looked and worked just like a chartreuse Mister Twister.

All plastic baits have jig heads for starters. (It's worth noting that heads as light as ⅛–¹⁄₁₆ ounce are commonly used in shallow-water baitfish imitations; it isn't all in the "jigging.") So the fly had to have its weight up front. Dumbbell eyes tied in the fashion of the Clouser Minnow (so that the hook rides upside down) made sense, too. Twisters have great action, so I chose marabou for the tail, with chartreuse Flashabou or Crystal Flash to match the glitter embedded in the plastic of the tube jigs. And the body needed to be tubular and fluorescent. Some experimentation led to Estaz, a relatively new type of bright-glowing sparkle chenille used in Great Lakes steelhead flies.

The fly's fuzzy glow resembles very closely the tube jig's fluorescence, and the weighted head, marabou tail, and glittery Flashabou do their best to keep up with its flash and action. The fly capitalizes on the tube jig's best features—bottom presentation, tubular shape, and soft texture—and the smallmouth's inexplicable attraction to fluorescent chartreuse.

A smallmouth caught on a Sparkle Grub, perhaps the most versatile fly in larger rivers and lakes.

While this fly produces in smaller, shallower waters, it is especially valuable in lakes, reservoirs, and navigable rivers. Here is where the jig fishers have always had it over the fly fishers; here is where this fly closes the gap.

I don't mean to imply, by the way, that this is the only pattern that fills the need for a grub fly on the open water: Holschlag's Hackle Jig and other grub-shaped imitations with soft hackle, marabou tails, and a lot of weight also work. The Sparkle Grub, as I've come to call this fly, has worked best for me—that's all.

Regardless of pattern, the most important element in a deep-water imitation is the capacity for "working" in depths of 20 feet and more. Replicating the forage, the crux of trout fishing notwithstanding, is simply secondary. That's why professional fishers have a gajillion plastic baits: They're matching structure and stain, not species of minnows.

SEARCH COMMITTEES

As discussed in chapter 11, an important dimension to fishing is covering spots where the bass might be. There's a lot of water out there. Day in and day out, drifting is definitely the best way to locate them.

The most convenient way to fish any fly from a drifting boat is simply to cast behind the boat, let out line, and add split shot until you feel it tapping on the bottom. Take in a couple feet of fly line, and drift. It certainly works, particularly when using streamers to imitate baitfish down 10–15 feet.

As noted in chapter 9, you can also fish the streamer ahead of the drifting boat. This requires a slow drift if the water is of any depth, and it's more work. But it's generally a more effective presentation, particularly if you're fishing highly defined structure.

Here's how to do it: Start with a 50-foot cast, slightly off-line of the drift direction. Let the streamer sink, and try to keep a reasonably tight line by gathering slack. Next, execute a slow retrieve, letting things speed up as the boat passes and the streamer rises from the bottom. The strip-pause-strip and slow-swimming retrieves described in chapter 9 are both effective techniques.

The Clouser Minnow is an excellent open-water pattern in general, and it can be particularly effective fished ahead of the boat. So is the body-weighted Marabou Matuka (see appendix C), which presents a broad profile typical of these open-water baitfish. Not only do these patterns get down quickly, they "work" even as they sink. Open-water smallmouths, particularly those feeding on emerald shiners and alewives, look for baitfish that drop out of the school.

Not surprisingly, crayfish imitations require a more deliberate retrieve than streamers. Again, a good presentation can be achieved by fishing ahead of the boat, working the fly in as you drift in that direction. The boat needs to be drifting slowly. (Don't hesitate, by the way, to drag an anchor on a short line to slow down the drift.) You also need to throw a fairly long line. That way there's time to hand-twist for a way before the boat, in effect, passes the line.

The best crayfish cast is ahead and slightly to the side of the drifting boat, generally by two to six rod lengths. (The latter distance is easy to estimate once you've done it a few times.) This cast will let you "fish" the crayfish fly as your boat drifts by the line, leader, and fly. The slower the drift, the more rod lengths you can cast to the side, and the more water you can cover.

Unlike a stream situation, in which the angler remains stationary while the water column flows by, a drifting boat finds the angler moving and the column stationary (or at least moving more slowly than the surface). The ultimate effect, however, is similar,

Just as stream fishermen often drift nymphs upriver, boat anglers can get more depth and a better drift by casting ahead and to the side of a drifting boat.

whether you are fishing upstream or "upboat": Avoiding the "straightening" effect of current or boat drift on the line leaves the fly drifting naturally and close to the bottom.

Current changes the above presentations because it represents the movement of the entire water column (with speed variations, of course), not just its surface, as with drifting on a lake. In fairly shallow water the fly will move with the boat; you can bounce bottom as you drift with minimal drag, though in fast, deep water the boat will get ahead of the fly. If that happens, the above approaches do apply.

In any case, line control is important (a stripping basket will prove invaluable). Not surprisingly, you'll find it useful to keep as much line as possible off the water, maintaining a straight line from the rod tip down to the crayfish imitation. Watch the point at which the boat passes the line. Strikes come here, just as they do right as a fly swings into the current.

As the boat drifts away, you can slip some line to the fly to slow its rise from the bottom. Everyone has some favorite manipulations for this part of the presentation in a stream. The same ones work behind a drifting boat.

Just remember that bass may be reluctant to chase crayfish patterns, so they aren't particularly effective for "searching." They need to be fished too slowly. Streamers make better searching patterns, although the bass may ignore them if they've got their heads buried in the rocks looking for crayfish. In that case, you may want to anchor, fish for a few minutes, then drift on to a new spot.

Enter the Sparkle Grub. A general forage imitation with the capacity to work with a brisk drift, it represents a happy compromise between streamers and crayfish. You still want to make a lengthy cast ahead of the drifting boat, but you can fish it with an eye toward covering various areas.

Whether drifting or anchored or, for that matter, fishing upstream in current, fish Sparkle Grubs and similar patterns as you would a jig. (I know; I wish there were a

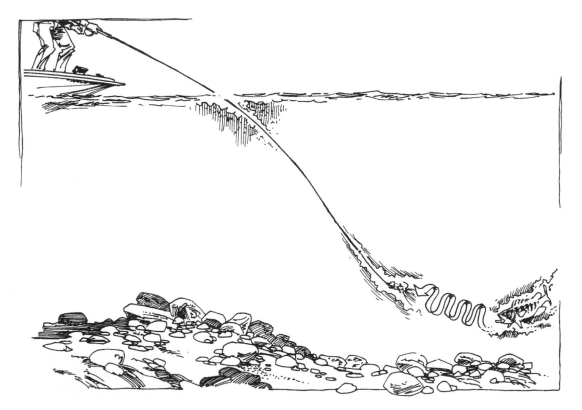

The best retrieve for a Sparkle Grub involves 3- to 4-inch strips with pauses in between. Try to keep the rod tip pointed at the water.

more delicate way to put it, too.) Bass often take on the drop, so watch the line carefully as the fly settles to the bottom. Once it hits the bottom, retrieve it in 3- to 4-inch strips, with the rod pointed right at the spot where the line enters the water. Keep the strips sharp, but not in rapid succession.

Pull the line over your index finger on the hand holding the rod. Rather than pinch the line as you would on a standard retrieve, let it slide back over your finger a little. This enhances the hopping motion of the fly while keeping the overall retrieve slow. You often set the hook inadvertently on the retrieve.

Once you target some fish, you may want to switch to a crayfish imitation, but don't be surprised if the Sparkle Grub keeps on catching them.

SMALLMOUTHS IN DEPTH

Drifting can be used to approach to targeted bass, too. Many larger lakes and rivers have shoals that can be measured in acres, and drifting often represents the best way to fish them. Ditto for scattered pockets of "micro" structures, such as gravel pockets, boulders, and weed patches. There's little point in setting up shop to fish each boulder or sprout of weeds.

When the fish are concentrated around a certain structure, or when the wind or current whisks the boat off too quickly for effective fishing, anchoring makes sense. But even then, some anglers prefer to make a series of drifts rather than anchor.

Last summer I fished with guide Allen Benas on the St. Lawrence River. Benas has a 30-foot boat; it's quite a production to anchor. He drift-fishes exclusively and catches all the bass he wants.

Allen lets me tag along once in awhile, as long as I stay up in the bow ("Gotta keep the riffraff away from my paying customers," as he puts it). The back of his boat is usually filled with anglers fishing live shiners which, if nothing else, certainly keeps me humble. On this particular day, Allen explained to the others that the weird-looking guy in the bow was doing research. Why else would anyone want to be fly fishing in 30 feet of water?

By midmorning I was glad for the cover. While his clients took bass, the fly rod up front was not doing so well. We'd been fishing on the outside edge of a large gravel flat in some 25–30 feet. I was having trouble taking anything other than a few sublegal bass and had run out of flies and excuses. I wasn't exactly recruiting new legions of fly fishers.

"I've got a couple small spots I want to try on the way in," Allen announced. "Reel up!" We roared out to the midriver shipping channel, a place I avoid in my 13-foot boat because of the parade of oceangoing barges.

Allen shifted into neutral upriver from the shoal buoy and gave us the game plan.

"O.K. Now this is a quick drift. When I say 'drop 'em,' let your bait go right to the bottom. We want to hit the side of the shoal, around thirty feet deep. The bigger fish are down there, not on top. Get ready."

He nudged the boat into gear, eyed the current, wind, and shoal, and then cut the engine. "O.K. Drop 'em!"

I cast a Sparkle Grub as far as I could ahead of the boat, then roll-cast some loose line to get more depth and tightened just as the boat approached. Glory be, I felt a weight. Then nothing, as the line rose to the surface. A beautiful 2-pound bass burst into full view.

I landed that bass and caught its twin on the next drift. Later, after fishing, I stopped at Allen's restaurant, and over a beer he told me, "You know, you hooked those bass in thirty-seven feet. That's what the graph recorder read." I've never caught a smallmouth on a fly in deeper water.

Most of us don't handle boats like Benas. Smallmouths in big rivers will hold on specific, highly defined structures, often in heavy current. So once you've located fish, anchoring is the most sensible strategy. The best approach depends, in large part, upon the preferences of the bass.

With crayfish the best technique is to fish upriver. An outfit that works for deep-water nymphing, which in a sense this is, works here as well. That is, a floating line with a long leader—much as described in chapter 7, in fact.

Depth complicates things, and in recent years I've experimented with a 2-weight running line, a section of Amnesia butt material, and a leader roughly as long as the water is deep (up to 22–25 feet long). The 2-weight cuts through the current (though hopefully you can keep line off the water), mends readily, and transmits a clear "bottom feel" as well. As with the standard floating line in shallower water, pinch whatever split shot you need to a dropper on the leader.

The trick with casting this rig is to flip it, casting the weight of the split shot, not the weight of the fly line. To do this, let 30–40 feet of line and leader hang below you in the current, but keep it on the surface. In the stripping basket or at your feet, you should have another 20 feet of line, or however much you want to shoot. The first step in the actual cast is to create a tension between the surface and the sinkers, then fling the rig, using the rod like a sling. You'd be surprised how far you can throw it, er, uh, cast it.

A two-weight running line, a section of Amnesia butt material, a 20-foot leader, and split-shot on a dropper is the best rig for drifting crayfish flies in deep (20 feet or more) running water.

If the bottom is littered with snags, the Sand Bag, a 2- to 3-inch length of parachute cord filled with lead, can be used with a snap swivel. But usually it's possible to "dribble" the split shot along the bottom by keeping a straight line between the rod tip and bottom.

With a Sparkle Grub, a drag-free drift isn't crucial or even desirable. So I use a High-D sink-tip with a 10-foot loop of lead core, a sinking leader butt, and a 3-foot tippet of 6-pound test. I wing it upriver as far as I can without seriously endangering those on board, then strip-pause-strip retrieve back with the current. I vary the casting pattern and sometimes begin the retrieve when the fly is opposite the boat. In short, I fish it like a Mister Twister on a jig head.

You can fish weighted streamers the same way, but when anchored in deep current you're probably better off fishing streamers in what amounts to an across-and-down presentation. It is very important to get the streamer near the bottom for at least part of the retrieve. You can pick up fish using the streamer retrieves discussed in chapter 9, adapting them to deep water. If you can get the streamer deep enough, simply holding it in the current and twitching it often tempts some bass.

Deep-water streamers in lakes and reservoirs can be fished this way, too, though I've never had much luck fishing streamers from a boat in deep water without a little motion of some kind—either from the current or from the wind. The hand-over-hand saltwater retrieve with frequent pauses is as good a retrieve as I know. Often I try to execute the pause around an obstruction—be it the key drop-off or boulder, or simply a strip of water where the bass seem to be hanging.

Keeping your fly near the bottom is tough when streamer-fishing from an anchored boat without current. It's one thing to do so with a crayfish imitation, which enjoys the

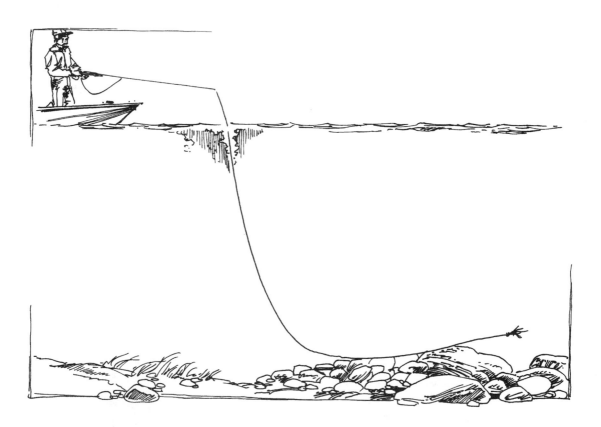

Fishing writer Ken Allen's deep-water brook trout presentation, in which he shakes out line to form an L, will keep your smallmouth flies closer to the bottom longer. This is a still-water presentation.

advantage of a slow retrieve, or with a Sparkle Grub, which has some weight of its own. But it's not easy to retrieve a streamer so that it swims along 20 feet down.

The full-sink line really helps, and so does a technique I learned from outdoor writer Ken Allen. Allen casts out and, while letting the fly sink to the bottom, shakes out more line so that it forms a sort of "L." This permits him to fish his streamer near the bottom for entire cast—a key concern when he's after big brook trout on some of Maine's backwoods lakes. The same strategy comes in handy for the open-water summer smallmouth angler.

The same retrieve, slowed down, works for crayfish in deep, still water, too. You just need to give the fly a chance to settle to the bottom. Take your time; retrieves in 20 feet of water should be slower than retrieves in 10 feet. With some patience, you can fish water up to 30 feet deep—when it's calm.

Still water often lets you get down with a sinking line and weighted fly and dispense with split shot or additional weight. Crawling a crayfish can be very effective, and you'll be surprised how infrequently you hang up as soon as you omit the split shot and fish with a crayfish imitation on which the hook rides up. I have a couple crayfish flies that I've used for two summers and haven't lost.

THE WIND

Wind is basically a pain in the ass. Fifteen miles per hour is about as much wind as I want to fight. More than that and I'm looking for a lee first, smallmouths second.

Casting is restricted to one plane: You want the wind blowing from left to right if you're right-handed, vice versa if you're left-handed. Most anglers who end up with a fly in an ear get it from overconfidence in a backwind. You want to watch those testosterone surges.

A stiff breeze seems to magnify the effect of weight in flies or on a leader. With weight you're probably better off (safer, too) casting into the wind—especially with the deep-water 2-weight crayfish rig, which you're actually flinging, not casting.

The wind also complicates boat control—it complicates everything, really. The trick, in perhaps overly simple terms, is to work with the breeze and avoid fighting it. Which is one of those wonderful little truisms that's far easier said than done, of course; I wouldn't even have brought it up were it not for the fact that bass often bite well under windy conditions, particularly in the hours before a storm.

If you can't find a lee, drift/trolling becomes an option. You may well need to drag an anchor to slow things down, and you may find, as I have, that the true limiting fac-

This angler drifted as a way of coping with windy conditions and hooked a nice smallmouth on the second pass over a gravel shoal.

tor is less presentation than hooking fish—difficult in deep water under any conditions and more difficult when wind is thrown in. In general, wind has the least effect on streamers, as hits on baitfish imitations tend to be solid. Sparkle Grubs can be trickier, crayfish and other bottom-crawling patterns toughest of all.

We do get more strikes than we realize. Reports from underwater observers universally confirm this notion. Paul Johnson has told of watching professional fishermen at work, of seeing 5- and 6-pound largemouth bass sucking in and spitting out lures even while they were being steadily retrieved. When this happened more than once, he left his underwater hideout and swam to the boat, intending to ask the fishermen why they weren't setting the hook. He emerged from the water at the boat and found them bored.

They wanted to go where there were some fish.

With crayfish patterns, this sort of behavior happens all the time. I'm convinced of it. Recall that smallmouths often take crayfish very tentatively in the first place. When you're crawling a crayfish fly across the bottom, some of the line and all of the leader crawl across the rocks, too. When depths are 15 feet and more and the wind leaves a chop on the water, a strike becomes all the more difficult to detect. Sometimes you'll feel a nip, most of the time resistance; other times the fish will just be there. You've got to set the hook hard, and I find it helps if you imagine trying to dislodge the bass from the rocks.

Smallmouths may take the Sparkle Grub more solidly. Sometimes the retrieve alone sets the hook. Strikes may also come as sharp pecks—like perch bites—or simply as solid resistance. Fish often take the Sparkle Grub (and the crayfish pattern) on the fall, and these takes are *really* hard to perceive.

COLD FRONTS AND BEYOND

Fly fishing often exists in an ideal world, and nothing can dispel that idealism quicker than a cold front on big water. The north wind blows and blows; the fly line ends up around your neck. And you don't catch squat.

Even bait fishers have a tough time. Bass will pick up hardshells and drop them in hopes of finding a softshell. My old buddy Pete Bellinger likes to dig out crayfish meat from the shell and fish it on a trout hook—a particularly scrumptious morsel presented in the most unobtrusive manner possible. Sometimes they want their grapes peeled.

Fishing can be tolerable right after a front, but it generally gets increasingly miserable as the barometric pressure rises and a high-pressure system takes over.

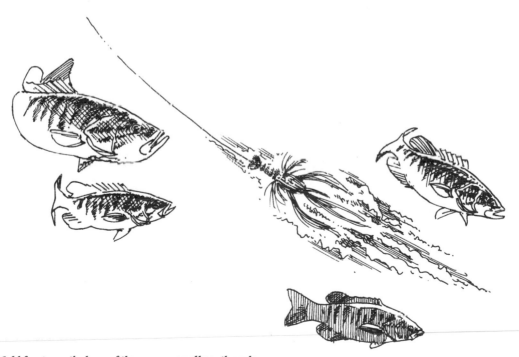

Cold fronts are the bane of the summer smallmouth angler.

There are various theories for this phenomenon. One is that the bright sun hurts the eyes of fish and causes them to remain inactive. Indeed, studies show that bass and crayfish are light sensitive. However, some of my best fishing has been on bright, sunny days—even in the spring, when fish are shallow. Light may have something to do with it, but it's hard to see it as the chief cause.

Another theory is that a shift in wind pushes the warmer surface water into different areas, leaving colder water in the spots where the fish were feeding the day before. So they shift locations. Perhaps. This theory does explain the observation that the best cold-front fish locations are slightly deeper.

Some anglers speculate about the impact of a pressure change on the lateral line of the fish, noting that high pressure puts a lot of force on the liquid of a lake. Perhaps this leaves the fish inactive and uncomfortable.

The inactivity effected by a cold front does not end with smallmouths, of course. Any fly fisher knows that warm, buggy nights make the best surface fishing. Underwater researcher Paul Johnson similarly connects gamefish activity with the overall activity of a waterborne ecosystem, noting how it varies day by day. This may be the final solution to the mystery of high pressure: Not only do the fish become sluggish with a pressure increase, but there's little food to be had anyway, since forage is largely inactive and not as available.

O.K. So this all sounded good to me, too. Then I spoke with researcher Mark Ridgway, who swims with the fishes, so to speak. As I asked him about the effect of cold fronts, I could hear him starting to laugh.

As a schoolteacher, I'm used to that. But most biologists are pretty polite. And Mark had always been very helpful to me.

"What's wrong?" I asked.

"You fishermen are always asking that same question. Now, what is it? When there's high pressure, the fish don't bite? Isn't that it?"

"Something like that," I said.

"Well, I'm sorry, but I've never seen any difference from one day to the next in how the fish behave."

I don't know about you, but I hate it when you can't find any evidence to support your theories. Not that such a problem ever stands in the way of fishing logic. We all know that the bass bite poorly after a front—at least they bite *our* flies and baits poorly.

So what works for fly fishing? Not much, to be honest. But Pete Bellinger's baitfishing tactics deserve a second look. The smallest crayfish patterns sometimes work. When they don't, I try to imitate a crayfish tail (though I doubt the smallmouths actually see that when they see my fly). Generally, something small, soft, and dark (or at least muted) in color. A Sparrow, a Casual Dress, even a Hare's Ear Nymph is worth a shot. It's interesting that this sort of scaledown in size, flash, action, and vertical presentation is typical of what professional bass and walleye fishers do during cold fronts as well.

Cold fronts are part of smallmouth fishing, of course; unavoidable, like going to the dentist. But they are just one part. There are grand times on the big water, too. When the breeze is soft from the south, the day fresh and new. Water-skiers out, their white plumes crisscrossing the blue-green waters. Air warm, sun bright.

* * *

The St. Lawrence is my home river, but it is only one of many major waters in the country that have splendid, bluewater fishing for smallmouths. The Great Lakes, the major reservoirs and lakes around the country, the defining waterways of the nation—this is the pulse of America's smallmouth fishing. For in its sum, deep summer on the open water resonates with what draws us to smallmouth fishing in the first place: complexity, precision, fertility.

Open-water smallmouths have survived mercury scares, the invasion of the salmon trollers, and the pestilence of the zebra mussels. They've been around for awhile. It was in the Great Lakes system, after all, during the late Pleistocene era more than twenty thousand years ago, that smallmouths originated. This is their homeland, so to speak. They fight like they know it.

Here in the Great Lakes system, smallmouth fishing is a way of life come summer. There's a rhythm to it all, and even people who don't fish comment on how the boats are off such-and-such a point or island now. Where the bass are biting becomes another way of marking summer.

The last time I saw Don Wolfe is a good example. It was in late August fifteen years ago at a decoy show he was judging. I went up and introduced myself, and he remembered me, remembered giving me advice on how to fish for bass. We didn't speak long; there really wasn't a lot to say. His eyesight seemed to be troubling him. He asked how my dad was. He said he wasn't surprised at all to hear that the bass were biting. He didn't bass fish himself anymore, but "this was the kind of weather you wanted, warm south winds in late summer."

There's a companionable dimension to summer smallmouth fishing on the big water, much as there is to waterfowl hunting. It isn't there with trout fishing—anglers usually each go their separate ways—and it isn't there with grouse hunting, either, as hunters consciously spread apart. So it is that trout fishers venerate their rivers and bird hunters their coverts. Waterfowlers, with all the work of setting up, with all the waiting and speculating, with all the time spent staring at the same seascape—they tend to recall their companions. Their nostalgia involves people, not places.

Late-summer smallmouth fishing on the biggest lakes and rivers has a different essence, more about floating in than connected to. A dreamy quality, silky, breezy, and warm, with days on the water that seem to reach forever in every direction. There is an aura of things and people past, of time suspended and blurred before the hard-edged industry of fall, of a last chance to stave off the dreaded world of work.

For now, the corn is high, and the weather fair, and tomorrow, with its obligations and looming expectations, seems far enough away that it really doesn't matter that much at all.

13

Closing Time

SEPTEMBER VACATION: Part I

Rain drummed on the van as my friend Stan Warner and I headed north on the Maine Turnpike. The last weekend in September, the final smallmouth trip of the season.

There were no uprooted trees or downed power lines as there'd been in Massachusetts. That was the good news.

We hoped the storm wouldn't work as far north as Lincoln, where we planned to fish the Penobscot River, out of "Dad's Camps."

Late in the afternoon, with rain giving way to a low, gloomy cloud cover, we reached the camp. The Penobscot was 300 yards wide here and boulder-studded, snaking through rocky shores dotted with yellow aspen.

We walked into the kitchen of the main cabin and into the smell of frying fish. A friendly, blond-haired woman waved us in.

"Smallmouths?" Stan asked.

"Oh no, white perch," she laughed. "We throw the bass back. You guys from Massachusetts gotta have *something* to catch after driving all the way up here." She dried her hands on her apron. "Hi, I'm Therese Thibodeau."

Ray Thibodeau came in from working on his woodpile and echoed Therese's sentiment: "Most people don't keep their bass. Which is great because it keeps this stretch of the river good fishing."

Fall offers some of the best fishing of the season, and chances are you'll have it all to yourself.

We asked for spots to try. "Doesn't matter," Ray told us. "The bass are everywhere. But I'd get started now. Looks like it might rain."

We still had a couple hours of light. Stan and I hurried down to the river's edge and launched his boat. I took the water temperature: 59 degrees. Not bad.

With a foot on the dock, I pushed us out into the current and watched for boulders as Stan kept us puttering across the river.

"No rain so far!" I shouted over the engine.

September is the first month of the school year. I cracked a beer and took a breath of Friday evening.

Fall Forage

Traditionally, outdoor activities fell into line with the seasons. Fishing season was over by September: Fall was for hunting and working. Muskies, which had to be fished in the fall, were the exception. Fall fishing remained vaguely unorthodox even into the 1980s.

Magazines used to run articles about the "Secret Season" and "Overlooked Fall Bonanza." But these days the word is out, and the overlooked dimension to fall fish, smallmouths included, is pretty much old news.

Not surprisingly, finding fall smallmouth locations depends on the available forage. The best fishing with crayfish and their imitations is over by early September. The dropping water temperature and decreasing light of autumn bring an end to molting. Meanwhile, young-of-the-year baitfish have finally reached a size that makes them worth pursuing. Smallmouths make a dramatic shift in foraging and, as Mark Ridgway has pointed out, begin feeding at an exceptional pace in order to survive the coming winter starvation and spring spawning seasons, their times of greatest stress.

To obtain maximum energy fall smallmouths increasingly key into the growing baitfish, following them along drop-offs or waiting in ambush along narrow guts and channels. Sharply defined humps and shoals surrounded by deeper water attract big schools of minnows and shiners, too. On larger waters, look to weedlines and shoals in 10–15 feet of water. Casting streamers and Sparkle Grubs along these structures on

Schools of smallmouths often move on to shallow shoals during the fall to feed on young-of-the-year baitfish.

bigger and deeper lakes and rivers can lead to very good fishing. A bonanza, you could call it.

A September fishing trip on the Connecticut River several years ago stands as a memorable example.

It was a mild evening with a few wispy clouds high overhead, and the sight of raindrops sprinkling across the river's surface simply didn't add up. I'm sort of an intuitive naturalist when it come to these things.

"Is that rain?" I wondered aloud.

"Can't be," my friend Ray Coppinger said.

He cut the engine, and the boat glided up to the "sprinkles." Fingerling bass skittered across the water. Hundreds of young-of-the-year largemouths (at least they looked like little largemouths, with distinct black lateral lines) swarmed over the shallow weed bed, which stretched across the river to the New Hampshire shore. They pecked at the glassy surface like fish in a hatchery pond.

A widely recognized biologist, one of the world's leading authorities on canines, in fact, Ray is the kind of guy who'll talk about wildlife biology until *all* the beer is gone. But get him in a boat and he's much more inclined to cast first and ask questions later. He immediately flung out a Panther Martin and hooked one of the small largemouths. It wiggled on the lure. Ray flicked it off into the river.

"There's your rainstorm," he said. "Maybe all these little guys will bring in some bigger fish."

"You've been watching too many fishing videos," I said. But worked out some line and a Marabou Muddler just in case.

"There's one!" Ray shouted, and the monofilament stretched out tight above the water. A dark smallmouth did a backflip out in the dusk. It was the first of more than a dozen fish we would catch that night, all from this same shallow weed bed, all within an hour, all on Panther Martins, and in my case, Marabou Muddlers, retrieved briskly just beneath the surface.

Earlier, we'd tried without success a sequence of deep-water spots: drop-offs, cliffs, bridge abutments, deep, rocky shores. The smallmouths simply hadn't been there. Instead, they were on the shallowest, broadest shoal in a six-mile stretch of river.

And there were 15- and 16-inchers in the bunch, good ones for this stretch of the Connecticut.

An orange moon rose above the northern Massachusetts farmland and hung in the clear night sky. We motored back to the launch; the air was alternately warm and cool as we skimmed over the empty river.

It was a fine night for a boat ride.

Big Bass

Article titles like "Fall Bonanza" may well be more appropriate than the editors who assign them ever realize. Fall smallmouth fishing really can be "a source of sudden great wealth or luck, a windfall," as the dictionary defines "bonanza." Like the night Ray and I fished the Connecticut. Nothing for the first two hours. But that third hour was really something.

Aside from prespawn, fall remains the best chance to catch big bass. If that's your goal, there are ways to narrow your odds. The most obvious is to fish the lakes and rivers that produce the prizewinners, information you can get from the appropriate state fishing award program.

Big smallmouths inhabit smaller waters, too. A number of years ago, on a mild September afternoon, my wife, Noreen, and I had an encounter with a truly large smallmouth in what may have been the smallest smallmouth pond I've ever fished.

It happened while we were eating lunch in the canoe, floating in a small bay. I'd rigged up a small perch on a bobber (well, I'd caught the *perch* on a fly, anyway), and when the float disappeared I thought I'd hooked a pickerel.

I reared back, and the biggest smallmouth I'd ever seen on *anyone's* line exploded from the water, topping out at eye level. It shook its head and the hapless perch popped out. I dodged the flying bait and it ended up, half scaled and still wiggling, on Noreen's lap.

It didn't stay there long.

Everything that could spill did, except for the canoe. I never saw that bass again, either, and it wasn't for lack of casting.

When I told bass fishing buddy Scott Johnson, who lived nearby, about it, he replied, "I didn't even know there were any smallmouths in there." Well, there were, and some of them—one anyway—were real beauties.

The profile of this pond goes as follows, and probably exemplifies trophy smallmouth habitat: little fishing pressure; some depth (60 feet in places) as well as shallow shoals of gravel and boulders; and perhaps most importantly, a forage base of crayfish.

The profile fits areas of larger waters, too. My friend Pete Bellinger and I have a spot on the St. Lawrence River near the International Rift where neither of us has ever caught a bass bigger than 15 inches before the end of August and, almost unbelievably, ever caught one smaller than 15 inches after.

I remember the evening we found this shoal. We were fishing with two other buddies, Ken Leon and Pete Loftus, and we'd been trying the bay side of an island for northerns. The anchor slipped off the ledge, and by the time it caught we were looking at some nice smallmouth water. Right in front of us.

I missed a fish on my first cast with a big white marabou streamer, the same one I'd been using for northerns. Meanwhile, Loftus tossed out a live crayfish and hung bottom, or so he thought, until a huge olive-bronze smallmouth leaped clear of the water. The fish sort of hung in the air, as if to pose for a picture, before belly-flopping back into the water. It used the current, turning broadside, taking line, shaking its head on the surface. In time, and with some excellent advice, Loftus landed a 22½-inch smallmouth, the only honest-to-goodness five-pounder I've ever seen come from the St. Lawrence.

As it turned out we caught six more bass that evening—all over three pounds; two topped the four-pound mark. I took one on a white streamer that came within an ounce of three-and-a-half pounds.

Over the years I've fished here quite a bit. It's not like I catch bass after bass. The seven bass we caught that first night were the most I've ever seen from this shoal. But the size of the bass I take is quite unusual for the St. Lawrence, where 13–16-inch fish are the rule.

What is there about this place? Who knows? On one side of the shoal there's a sharp drop-off with a deep weedline alongside. On the other there's a weed-filled bay with a number of islands. A strong current washes over the shoal, which itself is actually a 15-foot-deep gravel bar studded with boulders, rocks, old anchors, and who-knows-what else. For my baitfishing companions, every other cast ends up in an irretrievable snag. I've lost a few flies here myself. One thing is sure: When you approach this sort of shoal, you make your first cast count. Often as not the biggest bass will grab the first meal.

It's traditional in these sorts of "big-fish" discussions to include a reminder to check your knots and hooks. Persistence is another big one, championed as the secret to big fish. And it is important. Anyone who catches big fish with any consistency definitely puts in some time. But most of us don't have the chance to fish every morning or stay out on the water until we start growing tree moss. These days, I'm lucky if I get out a couple times a week.

A big bass, the really big one, fins at the heart of the fishing experience. But beyond fishing near the bottom in the fall in waters that hold big fish and doing so in the best spots you can find, there's not a lot to say about how to do it.

It certainly helps to know the river or lake you're fishing. Those who catch big fish consistently have the spirit of the water in them. Like Don Wolfe and the St. Lawrence

Trophy smallmouths can make fall fishing a memorable experience.

River. Or Bob Clouser and the Susquehanna, or Eddie Reif and the Penobscot. That's one possibility. But you either have it or you don't, and if you don't there's not a whole helluva lot you can do about it.

Professional anglers catch big fish, too. They do it by studying their quarry, checking their knots, sharpening their hooks, casting like machines, fishing dawn to dark every day. It's fashionable among fly fishers to worry that the competitiveness of tournaments threatens the pastime of fishing. Perhaps. But the guys who consistently catch trophy bass are also very good fishers. Their livelihoods depend on it.

You can emulate the discipline of professional anglers and probably catch more, bigger bass. But frankly, where you draw the line between discipline and fun in your fishing trips is really your business, not mine. Personally, I like knowing that I stand a chance of hooking a big one, and then relaxing and having a blast.

I've long since resigned myself to catching fewer trophies.

SEPTEMBER VACATION—Part II

As September becomes October, smallmouths drift to deeper water. By the end of October you'll find them as deep as 30–40 feet. Bass in smaller flows, rivers, and streams likewise migrate to the deepest, slowest water they can find.

The key is water temperature. It's commonplace to read or hear how smallmouths become reinvigorated in the cooling water temperatures of fall, but that's mostly fiction. The fast fishing of early fall is more a response to concentrated bait and intensified foraging than it is relief from heat or whatever other anthropomorphizing we come up with. Below 55 degrees and the fly fishing grinds to a halt.

Eddie Reif told me that he stops guiding on Maine's Penobscot during mid-September, less because the temperature is too low—it's usually still in the 60s then—than because of the procession of cold fronts that sweeps across the north country.

In fact, Reif had told me this two nights before Stan Warner and I left Massachusetts for Lincoln, Maine. It's never a good sign when the best angler on the river puts away his rods for the season.

But as we left the dock at Thibodeau's on the Penobscot, second-guessing our trip (which we'd done plenty of on the way up) was behind us. Things were looking up. No rain.

As I said, we dodged car-sized boulders on our way upriver to the foot of an island and began working weed beds with poppers and bugs. The evening just didn't have a topwater feel to it. A few white caddis struggled into the air, but with the cool, cloudy weather, no fish showed at the surface.

"Enough of these weeds," Stan said. "Let's try some structure."

We did, with Stan turning to live shiners while I experimented with various streamers, Sparkle Grubs, and Woolly Buggers. About an hour before dark we finally found some smallmouths—or rather Stan did. Drifting over rubble slightly out of the current in about six feet of water, he took six or seven in the 12–15-inch range on live shiners before I finally hooked one on a Woolly Bugger.

Then the rains came, first as drizzle, then steadily right at dark, and we maneuvered our way through the boulder maze back to the camp for a warm meal.

That evening, Thibodeau laughed when we asked if he'd heard tomorrow's weather report. "They call for rain," he said, "so maybe it won't."

Stan and I went to sleep with the sound of rain drumming on the cabin roof.

It was doing much the same in the morning. When it subsided, we made a beeline for the boat, trying first a spot upriver, then the area where Stan had taken the fish the night before. Nothing. Around 9 A.M. rain started up again, and the day turned dark.

An hour later it was raining harder, and we had yet to touch a fish. Things were not looking good for the visiting team.

Until this point we'd been anchoring near rocks in slack water between six and ten feet deep. Anchor, fish some, drift a bit, and so forth. Our thinking was that we needed to fish slowly near the bottom; that's how we'd taken the fish the night before. But now we maintained a full drift in order to cover more area.

Finally, Stan hooked a fish on a live minnow right near a weed bed. Then another. Then I took, one, two, three on a Sparkle Grub. The rain pounded. But we'd found fish—on the bottom, downstream from weed beds. It was all quite amazing.

It rained all day. The air temperature remained close to 60 degrees, though. This saved us from hypothermia and the bass from lockjaw. Over the course of the day we took more than fifty smallmouths, some forty of which fell to Stan's shiners, the rest to my streamers and Sparkle Grubs. I don't know as I've ever enjoyed ten smallmouth bass more.

We had to be home that night, as both of us had to prepare for Monday classes. So we quit at 5 P.M., loaded the boat, said goodbye to the Thibodeaus, and hit the road.

It stopped raining some two hours to the south, where I took over the driving while Stan took a nap. We drove across the bridges of the great rivers of southern Maine and New Hampshire—the Kennebec, the Androscoggin, the Piscataquis. To the east, over the Atlantic Ocean, the evening sky shone bright with the moon, and I could see white clouds pushed by a northwest wind.

The season was over. The trip, the six hours up, three hours back, and three hours still to go, had been—was still—quite worth it.

After my summer-long immersion in smallmouths, in writing this book and fishing the Thousand Islands, it was interesting to visit Maine, where locals, except for those whose livelihoods depend on it, continue to consider smallmouths an annoyance.

Several days later, after I returned, I mentioned our fifty-bass day to a friend who lived in Maine, and he said, "See, I told you they were a pain in the ass." Too bad he never got hooked up with a walleye fishing store owner I know in Vermont.

I guess in many ways, smallmouths-scorned-in-a-culture-of-trout is the story of my life. And over the years, the only thing it's ever made me want to do is catch smallmouths all the more. You could probably say that not being able to fish bass was what got me wanting to fish them in the first place. Wanting, more than anything else in my life, to become a bass fisherman.

Now don't get me wrong. As I mentioned earlier, I absolutely loved trout fishing with my dad. But I never thought about becoming or even being a trout fisherman. I mean, I was one, by birth.

The author and cousin Mike Bechaz heading out to Linda Island, circa 1961.

But a bass fisherman. That was something I could become on my own. It wasn't me to start with; it wasn't in my blood.

It's been that way forever. My earliest fishing recollections center around a picture in some book of a bigmouth bass, as they were known in those days, crashing up through the surface, lily pads draped across its back, all set to engulf a frog.

I was in kindergarten at the same time, and me and my friend Lee Ellsworth used to look at the book during naptime.

"We should catch some frogs and use them to catch bass," I announced.

"Sounds good to me," Lee said.

We spent the first part of the summer searching for big frogs and finally caught several, which we kept in a frog pen.

Waiting to go bass fishing.

But those days were a way off. My dad, after all, was a trout fisherman. Full-grown bullfrogs have never been known as particularly good brook trout bait. In fact, the brook trout we typically caught probably would have made good frog bait.

The next summer was a different story, as plans called for me to spend some time with my Uncle Frank and Aunt Margaret in the Adirondack Mountains. I was confident that I could get a couple bass trips onto the itinerary.

I decided to do some research that spring. About the only thing I knew about bass was that they were easier to catch than trout.

When pressed, my father admitted that fried bass fillets tasted good with beer, which as far as I could tell failed to distinguish them from other fish or fowl or, with the exception of a few inedible roots and barks, anything else.

And that if you were going to bass fish, you might as well go at night for large-mouths at Rutland Pond. He let that slip while he was cleaning the garage one day. He'd been holding out on me!

"Whaddaya use for bait?" Me and Lee had a new frog pond, and I thought the of-fer of some bullfrogs might result in an invitation to go along some night.

"Plugs," he said. "Crazy Crawler's a good one."

Crazy Crawler! Man, they had great names. "What color? What's it look like?"

"Frog-colored, like those frogs you and Lee catch down in the swamp. Here's one right here," he said, reaching into one of the old White Owl cigar boxes that lined the shelf above the stepladder. "A big bass broke the hook off. Just threw it over by the bull-rushes and lily pads on the south end, and he clobbered it. Here, you can have it."

I turned it over in my hand. Sure enough, it was colored like a frog. I tied some string on it and pulled it around in a washtub. The metal side paddles flapped back and forth, gurgling and all; it looked great.

"Hey Lee!" I screamed toward the upstairs apartment where his family lived. "Look what I got!"

Lee appeared at the screen window, then came clumping down the back stairs.

"If it's another frog, just put him in the pen. The last two got loose in my sister's room. She hasn't slept the last two nights and neither has my mother. I'm going to get sent to missionary school. That's what my mother keeps saying. I think she means it."

He pointed at the Crazy Crawler. "Hey, what's that?"

"It's just the best bass lure ever made," I said. "A Crazy Crawler. It works really well up at Rutland Pond at night, you know," as if I'd been using it there myself.

"Geez, it might work up at Brookside," Lee said, referring to the pond at the local cemetery, within easy striking distance of our bikes. It was loaded with bluegills. "Whaddya think?"

I thought it was a terrific idea. But when we tried it the next day, the Crazy Crawler sent the bluegills scattering for the shelter of the weed beds.

Still, what a possession: a frog-colored Crazy Crawler! It saw a lot of action that summer when I fished the Adirondack ponds with my Uncle Frank. No fish, but a lot of playing time.

My first real brush with a bass of any stature or size came quite by accident a cou-ple springs later, while bullhead fishing in a small creek that wound through the back acres of my uncle's farm not far from the St. Lawrence River.

There, one liquid April morning, with pungent marsh smells filling the air and blue-winged teal veering above the cattails, I had what, in retrospect some thirty-five years later, could only be described as a conversion experience.

Before it, I wanted desperately to go bass fishing; after, I simply had no choice.

Me and my cousin Mike and a cluster of other kids had spent the morning thinning the ranks of the pumpkinseeds, perch, and bullheads that spawned in the small creek. Cane poles and night crawlers were the weapons of choice.

When the noon whistle sounded, everybody scrambled up the bank and tore down the road to lunch.

Everybody but me. At that moment, my bobber dipped below the surface. I had to take care of this fish first. With two hands on the pole I began to lift it in, when suddenly, and quite definitely, it pulled right back.

Were a steelheading angler of today watching, he would say I gave that fish the "C" as I shoved out the butt end of the rod with my left hand and drew in the midsection with my right.

It was as if my brief but fantastic bass fishing life passed before my eyes; as if the bass leaping out of the muddy water right in front of me was leaping from a picture book. But it was not imaginary; this was not a drill. It was a goddamn, genuine, head-shaking black bass.

I realized it was a bass (in retrospect, a bigmouth, probably) just before it broke the line. When that happened, the whole marsh fell silent, just like when someone shattered a window with a baseball—such was my thought at the time.

The waves in the creek—the evidence, if you will—faded into concentric circles.

I plopped back down on the muddy bank and sat there for a moment watching the old black Dacron line float hookless on the softest of April breezes. I looked around. No witnesses. I knew what that meant.

When I got back to the house, no one believed me, of course. Uncle Joe winked at Aunt Anne and called me "quite a fisherman!" My cousin Don giggled and said I was "just like all the other city kids; thought I had a bite when I really had a bottom."

The whole episode taught me quite a bit. Notably, the ultimate futility of fish stories.

But it also started me down the road to a larger truth, one of those things that you never realize you know until later in life. In this case, much later, long after I'd tried to become the proud owner of a motorized lure and watched trophy smallmouths eat frogs in small Adirondack ponds. Long after I'd caught those smallmouth bass during the summers at Cedar Point with the help of Don Wolfe and talked my trout fishing dad into wallowing in a creek to help me seine crayfish, and even, I suppose, after I'd convinced nonfishing loved ones into going bass fishing.

In fact, I suppose I didn't really get it until after I'd caught many smallmouths over many summers.

It's this: The best part of fishing is the scheming and dreaming, not the landing and proving. I've never been a more intense bass fisherman in my life than during those primal days of fantasizing from the picture in the book, of trying to catch the biggest bullfrogs in the county, of trying to derrick in a 5-pound fish with fishing line ten times my age.

In the end what I wanted more than anything else was to catch a bass so that I could finally, once and for all, become a bass fisherman. It wasn't until I'd caught them for years and years and the whole thing had become quite predictable that it finally hit me.

I'd been one all along.

APPENDIX A

The Best Smallmouth Waters

The beauty of smallmouth bass fishing is its proximity to major population centers in the East, Midwest, and Northwest. Good smallmouth fishing, often as not, means stopping on the way home for a few casts or getting in an hour of fishing after dinner. Few of us can so characterize our trout fishing experiences. For most, travel and trout seem inseparable.

Some smallmouth areas do warrant special attention, however—whether because of tradition or the quality of the fishing. What follows is a humble attempt to summarize these destinations.

Although smallmouths swim in forty-nine states, the best fishing centers in five main areas: the Great Lakes system (including the St. Lawrence River and Lake Champlain); the Northeast, including New York and New England; the mid-Atlantic/Upper South/Ozark hills; the Midwest rivers and lakes; and the Northwest river systems.

THE NORTHWEST RIVER SYSTEMS

The best smallmouth fishing in the West is found on the river systems of Oregon and Washington. The Columbia River system has some very good fly fishing, not only in its main stem but in tributaries as well, most notably the Okanogan and Yakima Rivers and, in particular, the Snake, which has a reputation as an excellent float-fishing river.

In Oregon, the John Day River is another productive tributary of the Columbia. Many consider the Umpqua River system in southern Oregon the best fly fishing for smallmouths in the West. Like the Snake, it has a reputation as a terrific river for floating.

A number of lakes and reservoirs in Oregon (Oxbow Reservoir, Hell's Canyon Reservoir, Lake Owyhee, and Brownlee Reservoir) and in Washington (Banks Lake, Moses Lake, and Potholes Reservoir to the east, and Sammamish Lake in the west) offer good smallmouth fishing, too.

THE MIDWEST RIVERS AND LAKES

In Iowa, tributaries of the Mississippi, notably the Iowa River, Cedar River, and Volga River, all have smallmouths. In Illinois, smallmouths inhabit the Fox River, Rock River, and Kankakee River. To the east in Indiana, the Sugar River, Tippecanoe River, and Pigeon River all have good smallmouth fishing.

In general, the northern tier of the upper Midwest has the region's best smallmouth fishing. Smallmouths swim alongside the walleyes throughout the lakes and rivers of this region, and thus often go unnoticed. Lake of the Woods, for instance, has excellent smallmouth fishing, but it also proclaims itself the walleye capital of the world. It isn't difficult to figure out what everyone tries to catch.

In Wisconsin, flowages and lakes often have overlooked smallmouths, and certain rivers, notably the Wisconsin, St. Croix, and Mississippi, have good smallmouth fishing. To the east in Michigan, the Grand River, Kalamazoo River, St. Joseph River, and Muskegon River all offer fine smallmouth fishing.

Lakes in the shadow of Lake Superior, notably Grindstone Lake, Round Lake, Lac Courte Oreilles, Turtle Flambeau Flowage, and (a bit to the east) Lac du Flambeau, Crawling Stone Lake, Fence Lake, Tomahawk Lake, Trout Lake, Franklin Lake, and Butternut Lake are all worth considering. The same configuration occurs on the Upper Peninsula, with Portage Lake, Silver Lake Basin, Lake Michigamme, Michigamme Reservoir, Indian Lake, and Manistique Lake. In lower Michigan, other lakes that offer good smallmouth fishing include Walloon Lake, Burt Lake, Douglas Lake, Mullet Lake, Grand Lake, and Long Lake.

As is typical throughout Great Lakes country, the first lakes inland offer exceptional bass fishing (for both species, actually). But the real smallmouth news in the Midwest, aside from Superior and Michigan, is the Boundary Waters section of northern Minnesota.

Many anglers fish at Rainy Lake, a sprawling, tea-stained body of water with endless smallmouth structures in fairly shallow water (under ten feet, for the most part).

Other anglers take advantage of the lower lakes, ponds, and flows in the Boundary Waters Canoe Area, in which great float-camping trips with days of unbroken solitude and excellent fishing for smallmouths are possible. Trips of a variety of lengths can be arranged, and the area's canoe-only rule offers not only great smallmouth fishing but an uncommon tranquility as well. The surface fishing holds up throughout the season. A number of outfitters work this region, and calls to local chambers of commerce should point you in the right direction.

THE MID-ATLANTIC/UPPER SOUTH/OZARK HILLS

Nowhere is the pastoral nature of smallmouth fishing more in evidence than in the Ozark Hills of Missouri and Arkansas. This was a classic smallmouth area in the early twentieth century and there's still smallmouth fishing here, though, as you'd expect, it's not what it was in the '20s and '30s.

In Missouri, the Gasconade River, Piney Creek River, Current River, Jacks Fork River, Eleven Point River, and Black River are all good smallmouth streams. In northern Arkansas, Kings River, Crooked Creek, and the Middle Fork of the Little Red River still have smallmouth fishing.

Big smallmouths also come from areas east of the Mississippi, most notably reservoirs in Kentucky, Tennessee, and parts of northern Alabama. The most famous may be Dale Hollow Lake on the Tennessee/Kentucky border, although there is much water to fish on the Tennessee River impoundments, notably Kentucky, Pickwick, Wilson, and Wheeler Lakes. There are a number of reservoirs in East Tennessee and Kentucky as well, on such tributaries as the Clinch, Little Tennessee, and Holston Rivers.

Fly fishing on these reservoirs is uncommon. The rivers and creeks of Kentucky are another story. There is some good fishing on the Nolin River in the central part of the state and, in particular, on the Kinniconick and Tygarts Rivers in the northeast part of the state.

But the fishing here pales compared with the creeks and rivers to the north. These are the classic fly-fishing rivers, not only because of the good fishing they offer but because of the smallmouth fishermen associated with them: Harry Murray, the Shenandoah; Lefty Kreh, the Potomac; and Bob Clouser, the Susquehanna.

West Virginia has some top-flight smallmouth fishing. The turbulent waters of the New River provide excellent smallmouth fishing, and the whitewater float fishing can be exceptional. To the north, the Greenbriar River, Elk River, South Branch Potomac, and North Branch Potomac are good for smallmouths.

Four of the country's most fabled smallmouth rivers flow through Virginia and Maryland. The James River in western Virginia is a fabulous boulder-strewn float river that offers not only fast fishing but the chance at a trophy. The Rappahannock is a good smaller river; the Shenandoah, with its fertile alkaline flows and rich insect and baitfish populations, is a better one. Catches of fifty to a hundred smallmouths are not at all uncommon, although the average size will be smaller than on the James to the south or, for that matter, the Potomac to the north, given its deep, rich flows.

In recent years, the Susquehanna River in Pennsylvania has established itself as the top river in this region, not only because of the numbers of fish but because of their size as well. Limestone waters create a fertile flow, with a strong forage base of crayfish and baitfish. The water is shallow enough to be waded (in sections) and broad enough to withstand modern fishing pressure. As a result, fly fishers catch truly impressive numbers of smallmouths. Many anglers see Harrisburg as a good central location, by the way. As I said, it's not a wilderness experience.

THE NORTHEAST

The waters of New York and New England have some of the best smallmouth fishing in the country; as in the Pacific Northwest and upper Midwest, smallmouths often are overlooked in favor of other species. Darn.

The Delaware River, where it forms the border between Pennsylvania and New Jersey, is good and close to big cities. The Hudson River and waters in the New York water-supply system, notably the Ashokan Reservoir, offer some excellent smallmouth fishing, as does the Mohawk and its tributary, the Schoharie. Of the other Catskill rivers, the lower Neversink probably has the most to offer. To the west, the Unadilla and Chenanago are good bets; farther west, Lake Chautauqua and the Finger Lakes offer very good smallmouth fishing. In eastern New York, Sacandaga Reservoir, Saratoga Lake, and Lake George produce very good smallmouths. The same can be said of ponds and flows in the interior Adirondacks.

New England has some exceptional big-water smallmouth fisheries. Fly fishers can do very well in these waters. And when they don't, it's not due to a lack of fish.

In Connecticut, Candlewood Lake, a deep, clear body of water with a good population of alewives, produces numbers of smallmouths in the three- to five-pound range every year. To the north, Massachusetts has the Quabbin and Wachusetts Reservoirs, a pair of excellent smallmouth destinations. Wachusetts does not allow boats, so summer anglers often fish early in the morning and again in the evening, when the bass move in closer to shore.

To the north in Vermont, Harriman Reservoir, Somerset Reservoir, Lake St. Catherine, Green River Reservoir, Lake Seymour, and Lake Memphremagog all have fair-to-excellent smallmouth fishing (roughly in that order). In New Hampshire, Lake Winnipesaukee and Squam Lake are two clear-water smallmouth lakes worth exploring. Winnipesaukee offers more than 44,000 acres of fishing, with exceptional offshore shoals and islands. The transparent waters of Squam Lake have some very good angling as well. The state of Maine has exceptional big-water smallmouth fishing in, among others, Sebago, Belgrade, Sebec, and West Grand Lakes.

As elsewhere in the country, the lower stretches of all the region's trout streams provide topnotch smallmouth fishing. The great rivers of New England—the Connecticut (through its four states); the Merrimac in New Hampshire; and the Androscoggin, Kennebec, and Penobscot in Maine—have what might be the last untouched smallmouth fishing waters in the country. These waters (particularly the last two) offer excellent topwater fishing throughout the summer.

THE GREAT LAKES SYSTEM

The smallmouth's natal waters remain some of the best fishing. Smallmouths swim throughout the system. The best action on the American and Canadian sides of the lakes and rivers occurs in fairly shallow, rocky reefs, in water less than 30 feet deep for the most part. In some places fishing from tubes is growing in popularity; in shoals on Lake Michigan, for instance, it's possible to wade and fish. For the most part, though, fishing is a big-water experience best enjoyed from a substantial boat.

Despite its vastness, Lake Superior has the least to offer fly fishers; it's simply too cold, too deep. The waters of Chequamegon may be the exception.

Popular areas on Lake Michigan include the point of Wisconsin (including Green Bay), the Washington Islands, and, to the north, Little Bay De Noc and Big Bay De Noc. Garden Island, Hog Island, Beaver Island, and, in particular, Grand Traverse Bay are hotspots. The shoreline from the Indiana border 25 miles north to the town of Evanston—Chicago, in other words—offers excellent shore or boat fishing in harbors, piers, breakwaters, and riprap.

In western Lake Huron, the Les Cheneaux Islands are good spots, as are the Drummond Islands and the Canadian shores of Georgian Bay. In southern Huron, the waters of Thunder Bay have some exceptional bass fishing. Lake St. Clair is very good smallmouth water.

The western end of Lake Erie has a reputation as an excellent area for smallmouth fishing. The Bass Islands aren't called that for nothing. (This is my biologist friend Ray Coppinger's favorite bit of advice whenever anyone asks him for insights he might be hoarding about the intersection of animal behavior and fishing success: "Whenever you find anything named 'bass,' it's time to start fishing.")

Most of the other islands and structures in this region are well worth prospecting, too. To the east, the Canadian waters of Long Point Bay and all the waters east on both sides of the lake are very good for smallmouths, offering what could well be the best open-water smallmouth fishing in North America.

The Niagara River is one of the exceptional parcels of bass water in an exceptional bass system. The Upper River has a longstanding reputation, although the lower stretches of the river below Devil's Hole offer excellent smallmouth fishing during the summer.

There is some smallmouth fishing around the Rochester area of Lake Ontario, but on both sides of the lake the smallmouth fishing definitely gets better as you work east; the waters of Sodus Bay and Mexico Bay, as well as those on the Canadian shore east of Toronto, are quite good. The areas around Bay of Quinte as well as outside to Amherst Island are excellent fishing.

The timeless waters of the Thousand Islands region, from Stony Point east through Henderson, Chaumont, Hardscrabble, and Wilson bays to the River at Cape Vincent, are some of the world's greatest smallmouth waters. The outside shoals—Charity and Line Barrel, Duck Island, Stony Island, Galloo Island, and all the other grand offshore waters—are truly outstanding smallmouth spots.

The St. Lawrence has bass fishing for its entire length beginning at Cape Vincent, extending through the Thousand Islands downriver to Ogdensburg and Lake St. Lawrence and into Quebec.

The broad waters of Lake Champlain, which forms the boundary of New York and Vermont, offer some of the best smallmouth fishing in the Northeast. Champlain smallmouths can be found wherever there is a rocky bottom, although the most productive water remains north of the Crown Point Bridge. Smallmouths often stay near offshore shoals and steep shorelines where boulders have fallen into the waters.

The smallmouth spots above are well known, no secret certainly. As with any sort of angling, the fishing can fall off or improve with changes in the composition of fish populations, in water quality, in angling pressure, and of other conditions.

And, of course, the best spots to fish are the ones no one will tell you about. The only way to find them is go fishing.

It's a dirty job, I know. But somebody's got to . . .

APPENDIX B

Patterns, Presentations, and Water Types Reference Charts

WADEABLE STREAMS, (CANOE) FLOATABLE RIVERS, SHALLOW FLOWS

	EARLY SEASON Prespawn, Spawn, Postspawn	*MIDSEASON* Foraging, Schooling	*LATE SEASON* Energy Conserving
CHIEF FORAGE	aquatic nymphs, sculpins, darters, madtoms, miscellaneous	crayfish, sculpins, darters, madtoms, minnows, aquatic insects, leeches	young-of-the-year baitfish
LOCATION	deep areas with little or no current; gravel spawning areas out of current; slack water near shore	riffles, heads of pools (day), tails of pools (evening), beside boulders (day), near weed beds, near rocky shorelines	midwater weed beds, rocky shores, grass flats
TECHNIQUE	slow-drifting big wet flies and soft-hackled nymphs; poppers and bugs	dead-drifting in fast water with various nymphs and streamers; up and across with Bead-head Woolly Buggers; surface flies near obstructions and grass beds	popping bugs early; then streamers worked near current breaks of boulders, weedlines, and midcurrent grass beds
PATTERNS	black Woolly Buggers, Marabou Muddlers (deep); then poppers and hair bugs	hellgrammite imitations, stonefly nymphs, Bead-head Woolly Buggers, Muddler Minnows, Marabou Muddlers, hair bugs, poppers	poppers, Bead-head Woolly Buggers, chartreuse Sparkle Grubs, Clouser Deep Minnows, marabous and Muddler Marabous

189

NAVIGABLE RIVERS, RESERVOIRS, LAKES

	EARLY SEASON	*MIDSEASON*	*LATE SEASON*
CHIEF FORAGE	baitfish, juvenile panfish	crayfish, sculpins, darters, juvenile panfish, alewives, shiners, miscellaneous	young-of-the-year baitfish and panfish
LOCATION	drop-offs near spawning bays; rubble/gravel bays, 3–10 feet	midwater gravel/rock shoals, weedlines, mixtures of boulders/gravel/weeds, rocky shorelines, fallen boulders, cliffs, drop-offs	drop-offs, weed beds, points, shoals; later, deeper-than-20-foot flats with humps
TECHNIQUE	first, streamers on sink-tips over drop-offs; later, poppers and hair bugs	crayfish and Sparkle Grubs on bottom in gravel/rubble mixtures; streamers and Sparkle Grubs along weeds, drop-offs, cliffs, boulders	streamers in current breaks near obstructions and down-river from weed beds—also on and adjacent to shoals; later, streamers deep near drop-offs
PATTERNS	marabou streamers, black Woolly Buggers, white and yellow poppers, hair bugs	crayfish imitations, chartreuse Sparkle Grubs, Bead-head Woolly Buggers (rivers), Clouser Deep Minnows, Marabou Muddlers and marabous	marabou streamers, Sparkle Grubs, Clouser Deep Minnows, Clouser Ultra Deep Minnows (clear water)
NOTES		Shoreline structures (i.e., boulders, drop-offs) are often better in early morning; midwater shoals in the afternoon.	

GREAT LAKES SYSTEM

	EARLY SEASON	*MIDSEASON*	*LATE SEASON*
CHIEF FORAGE	juvenile panfish, available adult baitfish	crayfish, darters, lake shiners, alewives, and other available baitfish	young-of-the-year alewives, emerald shiners, and other baitfish
LOCATION	fairly deep water (20–35 feet); then along gravel and rubble shorelines in 3–10 feet of water	gravel/rubble offshore shoals in 10–30 feet; gravel boulder patches in weeds; cliffs with fallen rocks in water	drop-offs, weedlines, shoals in 10–15 feet of water; then humps and points in 20–25 feet
TECHNIQUE	first, streamers drifted in deep water; then marabou streamers cast on a sink-tip for spawn and postspawn fish	hand-twisting (in still water) and drifting in St. Lawrence and other currents; bouncing Sparkle Grubs along bottom; working streamers along weedlines	drifting; then anchoring and casting to schools with streamers and Sparkle Grubs
PATTERNS	white, yellow, and gray marabou streamers	crayfish imitations; chartreuse Sparkle Grubs; marabou streamers in white, blue, gray, and chartreuse; Clouser Deep Minnows in white and chartreuse	white and chartreuse Sparkle Grubs, white/silver marabou streamers, Clouser Ultra Deep Minnows
NOTES	Bass season may be closed during the prespawn and spawn, depending upon location.	Express rate, full-sink, and sink-tip lines are very important. Summer fish, except those relating to grass, are deep.	Some anglers think that cold fronts have less influence during fall (I'm not one of them).

Fly Patterns

$\mathbf{T}$he flies included in these plates aren't necessarily the best thirty smallmouth flies. They are simply flies that have made their mark as smallmouth bass flies, as opposed to trout flies suitable for smallmouths. Admittedly, the Messinger Bucktail Frog and Most Whit Hair Bug are used just as widely for largemouths as for smallmouths. But few other bass bugs are so popular with smallmouth anglers, hence their inclusion in these plates. The full list includes trout flies used as bass flies.

PLATE 1: Floaters and Swimmers

1. Tap's Bug

Tail: Deer hair

Body: Deer hair

Designed by H. G. Tapply; tied by the author.

2. Sneaky Pete

Tail: Four splayed hackle feathers

Hackle: One or two hen feathers

Legs: Rubber hackle, two facing forward, two facing backward

Body: Cork cylinder, reversed, with wide end facing rear and tapered end facing forward

3. Dahlberg Diver

Tail: Mixed hackles (four), Flashabou or Krystal Flash, and marabou

Hackle: One or two marabou or saddle hackles wound on

Collar and head: Spun deer hair clipped to shape—flat on the bottom, collar in back, and tapered to a point at the eye of the hook

Designed by Larry Dahlberg. All sorts of color combinations are used with this fly. It is arguably the most important surface swimmer today.

4. Whitlock's Damsel

Wing: Kingfisher blue and natural deer hair

Underbody: Foam

Body (including head): Kingfisher blue bucktail underneath and dark blue bucktail on the back, tied with tips facing forward and then pulled back to form a bullet head and extended body

Rib: Dark blue thread

Eyes: Hollow plastic

Designed by Dave Whitlock.

5. Messinger Bucktail Frog

Rump: Green deer hair on top, yellow on bottom

Legs: Green bucktail on top, yellow on bottom

Body: Green deer body hair on top, yellow and white on bottom

Eyes: Plastic, painted

This is the original pattern designed by Joe Messinger Sr. and tied by Joe Messinger Jr. This imitation has remained virtually unchanged for seventy-five years and has accounted for countless big bass. The legs are the complicated part of this tie. Basically, heavy thread and a straight pin are included inside the bucktail. The bucktail is tied to the pin and thread. The pin is then bent and trimmed and the joint cemented. This is a complex tie, so much so that Joe Messinger Jr. offers a video on it: "Tying the Bucktail Frog with Joe Messinger." This video may be purchased for $39.95 from Joe Messinger Jr., Rt. 9, Box 119-M, Morgantown, WV 26505. There is also an excellent description in *Bug Making* by C. Boyd Pfeiffer.

6. Swimming Frog

Legs: Mix of marabou, hackle feathers, and Flashabou or Krystal Flash

Feet: Rubber hackle

Body: Deer hair, green on top, white or yellow on bottom, clipped to shape— rounded on top, flat on bottom

Eyes: Plastic

On this and other hair bugs, I generally apply considerable flotant to the underside to keep the bug on the surface.

7. Most Whit Hair Bug

Tail: Marabou, Krystal Flash, rubber hackles (two), outside of which are four splayed hackle features (two on each side)

Hackle: Soft hen hackle, wound on

Legs: Rubber hackle

Body: Spun deer hair

Eyes: Hollow plastic

Designed by Dave Whitlock.

8. *White Fly*

Tail: White deer hair

Body: White fur

Wing: White deer hair

Hackle: White

If you wish to work this fly aggressively, tie the hackle thorax-style and keep it bushy.

Dry flies not pictured:
1. Irresistible
2. White Wulff
3. Hair-winged Royal Coachman
4. Devil Bug
5. Humpy
6. March Brown

Bugs and poppers not pictured:
1. Cork Popper
2. Gerbubble Bug
3. Lefty's Bug
4. Pencil Popper

PLATE 2: Streamers

9. *Clouser Ultra Deep Minnow*

Eyes: Secured to the top of the hook so that fly rides upside down. Use Super-glue or other CA so that eyes do not twist.

Underwing: Light chartreuse Ultra Hair tied on top of hook

Overwing: Light chartreuse Ultra Hair, over which is light-colored Krystal Flash and light chartreuse Ultra Hair

Designed and tied by Bob Clouser. The entire Clouser Minnow series is well worth including in any fly selection. Given the increasing clarity of lakes these days (in particular the Great Lakes, because of the influx of zebra mussels), the Ultra Minnow is a great addition to a streamer collection designed for smallmouths. Clouser notes that it is his favorite pattern for fall, when smallmouths turn to baitfish and rivers often run low and clear.

10. *Marabou Shiner*

Body: Silver Mylar or Corsair tubing

Wing: White marabou, over which are a few fibers of purple marabou and electric blue Krystal Flash. Next come a few fibers of yellow marabou, followed by a bit of chartreuse marabou, topped with gray marabou. Silver Flashabou should be mixed with gray marabou. Peacock herl topping is optional.

Head: Fire red next to body, followed by gray thread

Eyes: Small stick-on. Entire head can be coated with high-gloss cement, which gives the fly a nice shine and protects the eyes.

Tied by the author. A. W. Ballou designed the first marabou streamer as a land-locked salmon pattern back in 1922. Bob

Zwirz was the first to add flash to the wing, with the Miracle Marabou of the early 1960s. I like flash wherever I can get it in a streamer. Corsair tubing is my current heartthrob. I tie an inner body of holographic (3-D) tinsel. It's probably not worth bothering with unless you enjoy fussing with materials.

11. Marabou Thunder Creek

Body: Gold Mylar tubing

Wing: Black, brown, and white marabou and gold Flashabou

Head: Reversed marabou

Eyes: Adhesive, pearl background, black center

Throat: Fire red thread

Cement: Vinyl, undercoat; head cement, intermediate; high-gloss, surface

The Thunder Creek style was designed by Keith Fulsher. This fly was tied by the author.

Tie in the gold Mylar tubing body. Turn the hook in the vise and tie in the white marabou below the hook at the eye. The fibers should extend the length of the body beyond the hook eye. Turn the hook right-side up and add gold Flashabou. Tie in a thin pinch of black marabou on the very top of the hook (when pulled back this will be the top of the fly). The fibers should extend the length of the body beyond the hook eye. Tie in the brown marabou (a bit more than the white marabou) on the top of the hook, so that it covers the black marabou. The fibers should extend the length of the body beyond the hook eye. Leave a strand of

thread ¼ inch behind the eye. This will be the tie-off spot for the head.

Turn over the fly, and pull back the white marabou first and tie off ¼ inch beyond the eye. Turn the fly right-side up and pull back the brown marabou, tying off. Stroke fibers carefully to form the color separations. Next, pull back the black strip, again taking care to keep the color separations. Finally, pull back the Flashabou and tie it off with brown marabou. Give the head one coat of vinyl cement and one coat of enamel head cement. Press on adhesive eyes while the enamel is tacky. Let it dry overnight and add a few wraps of fire red thread for gills, followed by two coats of high-gloss.

The wing is the trick with this fly, obviously. Take your time when you first secure the marabou and Flashabou to the hook, and take your time when stroking them back to form the head. Pull back the Flashabou last so that when cemented, it gives the appearance of shiny gill plates. At first the head may look a little fuzzy because the fibers are reversed. Clip with scissors if necessary. When cemented they should lie down.

Many patterns can be tied Thunder Creek–style. I use this pattern to mimic a floating gold Rapala.

12. Marabou Matuka

Wing: White marabou, silver or pearl Flashabou; blue or purple marabou, with corresponding Flashabou; chartreuse marabou with chartreuse Flashabou; olive marabou with green Krystal Flash

Body: White rabbit mixed with white Lite Brite

Gills: Bright red sparkle floss

Thread: Olive

Eyes: Small adhesive. Head coated with high-gloss cement.

Designed and tied by the author.

Tie in the marabou in actual sections of the feather. (It's important not to start the Matuka over the hook, by the way. Otherwise it will wrap around the bend during the retrieve.) Next tie in Flashabou—two strands for each color clump. Cement, then dub the body, making as many windings between fibers as possible, which makes the marabou and Flashabou appear to sprout from the body. Wrap red sparkle floss for gills, attach the eyes, then give the head two coats of high-gloss head cement.

This fly takes awhile to tie, but it is surprisingly durable and an excellent deep-water imitation.

13. Sculpin/Darter Marabou Muddler

Underbody: Lead wire

Body: Light hare's ear, olive Antron, golden Lite Brite

Wing: Speckled olive and brown marabou, with brown and golden Flashabou

Collar and head: Mixed natural, olive, and brown deer hair, trimmed to shape

Tied by the author. This pattern is a derivative of the Marabou Muddler, one of the all-time great smallmouth flies. It can be tied without weight to be fished near the surface. This particular pattern uses sculpin/darter materials and colors and does its best work near the bottom.

14. Woolly-headed Sculpin

Body: Cream yarn, with yellow Lite Brite

Wing: Speckled brown feather, tied Matuka style

Pectoral fins: Small brown throat feathers from a ruffed grouse

Head: Brown lamb's wool

My buddy Ray Coppinger walked into the Orvis store in New York City and said, "My friend is writing a book on fly fishing for smallmouth bass, and I want to buy him the hottest smallmouth pattern you have in stock." This is the fly he was sold.

Streamers not pictured:
1. Marabou Black Ghost
2. Nine-three
3. Black-Nosed-Dace
4. Gray Ghost
5. Red and White Streamer (Kreh)
6. Lefty's Deceiver
7. Olive Matuka
8. Purple Zonker
9. Black Zonker
10. Whitlock's Prismatic Shad
11. Whitlock's "Match the Minnow" series
12. Hornberg
13. Nix's Shinabou Shiner

14. Muddler Minnow (and its many variations)
15. Clouser Deep Minnow
16. Clouser Foxee Deep Minnow

PLATE 3: Nymphs

15. *Clouser Swimming Nymph*

Tail: Marabou or rabbit fur to match body, with matching Flashabou

Underbody: Lead wire

Body: Mix of synthetic brown and brown rabbit fur

Covert: Peacock herl

Thorax: Same as body

Legs: Henback feather

Designed and tied by Bob Clouser.

16. *Brooks' Stonefly Nymph*

Underbody: Lead wire

Tail: Small bunch of grouse feathers

Body: Brown fur—mix of Antron, hare's ear, fox fur, and dark brown rabbit

Hackle: Brown grouse

Fly designed by Charles Brooks and tied by the author. This fly is a modification of the original tie (Brooks' Montana Stone), which was designed to imitate large black stonefly nymphs of rough-and-tumble western trout rivers. The dark brown colors are closer to stonefly nymphs common to smallmouth rivers, and the fur and soft hackle work better in the slower currents characteristic of smallmouth habitat.

17. *Sparrow*

Tail: Reddish brown marabou from a ringneck pheasant rump

Body: Olive rabbit and gray squirrel

Hackle: Several wraps of ringneck pheasant rump feathers

Collar: Filoplume from pheasant rump feathers

Designed by Jack Gartside; tied by Tim Roller.

18. *Turkey Feather Stonefly Nymph*

Tail: Condor barbules or stripped goose quill

Underbody: Cream fox fur mixed with hare's ear and golden Lite Brite

Overlay: Dark brown turkey

Rib: Brown floss, monochord, or Larva Lace

Abdomen: Cream fox fur mixed with hare's ear and golden Lite Brite

Covert: Folded dark brown turkey

Hackle: Brown grouse

This stonefly nymph is really a conglomeration of many patterns. It is not tied "in the round" like a Charles Brooks tie, and it is also more elaborate. It basically came about because I needed to do something with all the wild turkey tail feathers my friends started giving me back in the early '80s when turkeys made such a comeback in Vermont.

19. Art's Casual Dress

Tail: Gray and tan rabbit fur, tied heavy

Body: Brown beaver fur

Rib: Pearl Krystal Flash or Flashabou

Collar: Gray and tan rabbit fur

Head: Dark brown beaver fur

Eyes: Melted monofilament

Designed and tied by Art Scheck. Art writes: "This fly is an obvious rip-off of Polly Rosborough's 'Casual Dress' pattern (which ain't no slouch as a smallmouth fly, by the way). The tail and collar are bunny fur, the body is whatever gray/brown/tan crap you have lying around, the rib is six strands of Krystal Flash twisted together, and the eyes are melted mono. God only knows what the fish think it is—maybe a dragonfly nymph, maybe a sculpin, maybe a lot of bunny fur on a hook. But they like it. When I fish this mess in a river, I generally sling it upstream and strip slightly faster than the current to give the fur a little action. It's uncommonly effective."

20. Murray's Hellgrammite

Underbody: Lead wire

Tail: Black ostrich herl

Body: Black chenille

Hackle: Soft dark dun

Feelers: Black rubber hackle

Designed by Harry Murray; tied by the author.

21. Furry Hellgrammite

Tail: Small black rabbit strip, with black and olive Krystal Flash

Body: Mixed black rabbit and olive Antron

Rib: Black hackle, clipped on top and bottom, or black ostrich

Thorax: Mixed black rabbit and olive Antron

Legs: Soft black hackle

Wing cases: Dark turkey

Pincers: Dark turkey

Designed and tied by the author.

22. Bead-head March Brown Bugger

Tail: Speckled olive and brown marabou, with brown and copper Flashabou

Body: Brown Antron mixed with cream fox fur

Hackle: Brown grouse

Head: Brass or copper

This March Brown pattern has been an effective Woolly Bugger, although black, purple, and chartreuse also work well. It does an excellent job as a sculpin/darter imitation, and it also imitates a crayfish, perhaps, and a number of the larger nymphs that appeal to smallmouths. The mottled-brown color pattern may well be an important trigger to smallmouths; the soft materials—i.e., grouse hackle, fur, and marabou—most certainly are.

Nymphs not pictured:
1. Gold-ribbed Hare's Ear
2. March Brown
3. Montana
4. Bitch Creek
5. Bead-head Caddis
6. Sparkle Pupa
7. Zug Bug
8. Tellico
9. Red Squirrel
10. Clouser's Hellgrammite

Wet flies not pictured:
1. Gray Hackle
2. Brown Hackle
3. Black Woolly Worm
4. Yellow Woolly Worm
5. Olive Woolly Worm
6. Brown Woolly Worm
7. Light Cahill
8. Black Gnat

PLATE 4: Crayfish, Grubs, and Leeches

23. Schley's Crayfish

Head: Brown deer hair, spun and clipped

Pincers: Brown bucktail

Body: Brown chenille

Tail: Brown deer hair, spun and clipped

Designed by Ben Schley; tied by the author. In 1982, Schley published an article in *Fly Fisherman* magazine that put crayfish imitations on the map. Schley's chenille-and-bucktail pattern proved a good one, easy to dress and quite productive. It continues to be very popular today.

24. Clouser Crayfish

Underbody: Lead wire mounted on each side of the hook shank

Antennae: A few ringneck cock pheasant tail feather barbules

Nose: Tip of a hen mallard flank feather on top of antennae

Claws: Hen mallard, cut to shape

Body: Light gray yarn

Legs: Cree or mixed ginger and grizzly

Caraspace: Olive Furry Foam

Rib: Gray thread

Designed and tied by Bob Clouser.

25. Softshell Crayfish

Keel: Two strips of lead wire

Underbody: Fox fur and rabbit fur mixed with Antron

Claws: Small bunches of fox or rabbit fur with guard hairs

Legs: Grouse breast feathers

Caraspace: Olive, sandy, gray, or brown bucktail

Cement: Dave's Flexament

Designed and tied by the author.

Place the hook in the vise. Secure two strips of lead on top of the shank for the keel (this will keep the hook upside down). Cement and wrap the thread.

Flip the hook in the vise so that it's upside down. Tie in bucktail strands by the tips at the bend. (Make sure they are long enough to be tied back over the hook with the butt ends extending past the eye.) Tie in dubbing and dub the cephalothorax of the fly. Tie off, keeping the thread (with some dubbing) still attached. Then tie in the fox fur claws and wind on the grouse hackle legs. Next, wind on reserved dubbing from the thorax, crisscrossing the claws and gathering the grouse fibers into bunches. This section should be tied fat.

Pull the bucktail back tightly, keeping it spread over the upper half of the thorax. Tie down tightly just past the grouse hackle legs, and cement the winding. Add a strand of monochord (I tie in two in case one breaks), tie in the thread with the spun fur, and dub the abdomen. Pull back the bucktail, tying off at the eye. Rib tightly with monochord to create segments. Cement the entire bucktail caraspace.

To finish the fly, clip the tail and pick out the fur.

bra mussels. Here and elsewhere, bigwater summer smallmouth fishing demands a softshell crayfish imitation, and this pattern is the result of extensive scuba and fly-fishing investigation work.

Note, in particular, that claws are only hinted at in this imitation (by teasing out the Angora goat). Long explains, "Angora goat is best applied with a dubbing loop. Tease out with bodkin after wrapping. Lead eyes are attached to the top of the hook shank so that the fly rides with the hook up. The fly has an ethereal translucence when wet. Gets better as it fuzzes up with use. Angora goat is a Wapsi product and colors are numbered. To make a perfect Midwest softshell color mix (that works in the clear waters of the Great Lakes): #030 light gray (40 percent); #060 light olive (60 percent)."

26. BossBob's Dubbed Crayfish

Tail weight: ⁹⁄₃₂-ounce lead eyes, mashed flat with pliers

Feelers: Filoplume and bucktail

Caraspace: Furry Foam

Eyes: Umpqua Mono Eyes

Body, legs, and claws: Angora goat

Rib: Fine copper wire

Designed and tied by Bob Long Jr. Author of a number of fly-tying magazine articles, Long has been experimenting with crayfish patterns in the Midwest for some time. His most recent efforts have focused on the clear-water conditions of Lake Michigan since the appearance of the ze-

27. BossBob's Leech

Eyes: Umpqua painted lead eyes

Tail: Black rabbit strip with four strands of FireFly Synthetic Flash material

Body: Black chenille

Hackle: Soft black feather

Weedguard: Mono loop (20–25 pounds)

Bob Long Jr. designed this fly for fishing the leech-filled smallmouth waters of the Midwest. The eyes should be tied on top of the shank so that the hook rides up. Bob notes that the weedguard is optional and that the fly works particularly well for "bigger fish in low light (late-evening-into-night) conditions."

28. Sparkle Grub

Tail: Chartreuse marabou and chartreuse Krystal Flash

Body: Chartreuse Estaz

Eyes: Red with black center, attached Clouser-style on top of hook so that it rides upside down. Use CA cement so that the eyes won't twist.

Designed and tied by the author. White, yellow/brown combination, black, and purple are also effective (roughly in that order), although chartreuse seems to work in all water stains.

Crayfish, grubs, and leeches not pictured:
1. Yarrington's Swimming Crayfish
2. Joe Robinson's Mud Bug
3. Crawfish Shedder (Howey)
4. Holschlag's Hackle Jig
5. Dave's Lectric Leech

Bibliography

Aggus, Larry R. "Food of Angler Harvested Largemouth, Spotted, and Smallmouth Bass in Bull Shoals Reservoir." *Proceedings of Annual Conference of Southeastern States Fisheries and Wildlife* (1972). Nymph-eating smallmouths in a southern reservoir.

Allen, Ken. "Fishing Deep Water Brookies." *American Angler* (January–February 1991): 24–27. Excellent discussion of techniques for fishing deep-water streamers.

Applegate, R. L., J.W. Mullan, and D. I. Morais. "Food and Growth of Six Centrarchids from the Shoreline Areas of Bull Shoals Reservoir." *Proceedings of Annual Conference of Southeastern States Fisheries and Wildlife 20:* 469–82. Feeding habits of juvenile smallmouths.

Austen, Douglas J. and Donald J. Orth. "Food Utilization by Riverine Smallmouth Bass in Relation to Minimum Length Limits." *Proceedings of Annual Conference of Southeastern States Fisheries and Wildlife Agencies 39* (1985): 97–107. Feeding habits of stream smallmouths.

Bergman, Ray. *Just Fishing*. New York: Penn Publishing, 1933. Classic writing on the state of smallmouth fly fishing in the first four decades of the twentieth century.

———. *Fresh-Water Bass*. New York: Penn Publishing, 1942. Ditto.

———. *Trout*. New York: Penn Publishing, 1938. One of the most influential trout fishing books ever written.

Blades, Williams. *Fishing Flies and Fly Tying*. Harrisburg, PA: Stackpole, 1951. Extensive listing of early imitative smallmouth flies.

Brooks, Joe. *Complete Book of Fly Fishing*. New York: Outdoor Life, 1958. Some early material on fishing deep for smallmouths.

Brown, Arthur V. and Lloyd C. Fitzpatrick. "Life History and Population Energetics of the Dobson Fly, Corydalus Cornutus." *Ecology* 59(6) (1978): 1091–1108. Useful information on the life history of the hellgrammite.

Carlander, Kenneth D. "Community Relations of Bass in Large Natural Lakes." In *Black Bass Biology and Management*. Washington, DC: Sport Fishing Institute, 1975.

———. *Handbook of Freshwater Biology*. Ames, Iowa: The Iowa State University Press. Partial bibliography.

Caucci, Al and Bob Nastasi. *Hatches II*. New York: Lyons & Burford, 1986.

Coble, Daniel W. "Life History and Biology of the Smallmouth Bass." In *Black Bass Biology and Management*. Washington, DC: Sport Fishing Institute, 1975. Good life history with useful bibliography.

Engels, Victor. *Fishing in the Adirondacks in the 1930s*. Syracuse: Syracuse University Press, 1978. Wonderful tales of wilderness fly rodding for smallmouths.

Flick, Arthur. *Streamside Guide to Naturals and Their Imitations*. New York: Putnam, 1947. Groundbreaking work on imitating natural insects.

Field & Stream. Various issues, 1955–75.

Fly Fisherman. Various issues, 1972–present.

Fuller, Thomas. *Underwater Flies*. Camden, ME: Ragged Mountain Press, 1996. Excellent account of fishing beneath the surface for trout.

Green, David M. "The Importance of Yellow Perch in the Food of Predator Fish in Canadarago Lake." *New York State Fisheries Investigation Project* (1978). An extremely interesting study of the significance of yellow perch and darters in the smallmouth's diet.

Hafele, Rich. "Crayfish." *American Angler* (Spring 1988): 20–23, 72–74. An informative overview of crayfish biology; includes dressings for a variety of crayfish imitations.

Henshall, James. *Book of the Black Bass*. Cincinnati: Robert Clarke, 1881. The King James Version.

Holschlag, Tim. *Stream Smallmouth Fishing*. Harrisburg, PA: Stackpole, 1990. Solid how-to information on fishing in flowing water; includes various methods.

In-Fisherman. Various issues, 1980–present.

Fly Fishing Quarterly. Various issues, 1985–present.

Jaworoski, Ed. "The Swimming Nymph." *Fly Fisherman* (May 1990): 42–43. Discussion of tying and fishing the Clouser Swimming Nymph.

Jennings, Preston. *A Book of Trout Flies*. New York: Derrydale, 1935. Important book on imitating trout foods.

Johnson, Paul C. *The Scientific Angler*. New York: Charles Scribner's Sons, 1984. Some useful information on how fish respond to artificial lures and atmospheric changes.

Kreh, Bernard "Lefty." "Clouser's Deep Minnow." *Fly Fisherman* (July 1989). The Clouser Deep Minnow goes prime-time.

Latta, W. C. "Dynamics of Bass in Large Natural Lakes." In *Black Bass Biology and Management*. Washington, DC: Sport Fishing Institute, 1975. Interesting overview of the bass in big water.

Laszlo, Phelps T. "The 'Sparrow.'" *The Roundtable* (November–December 1976). Introduction of the Sparrow.

Ledlie, David. "The Black Bass in Maine." *The American Fly Fisher* 9, no. 3 (1982) 7–9. Fascinating excerpts from the nineteenth-century's fisheries commission's decision to stock smallmouths.

Lincoln, Robert Page. *Black Bass Fishing*. Harrisburg, PA: Stackpole, 1952. Some information on fly fishing for smallmouths.

MacCrimmon, Hugh R. and William H. Robbins. "Distribution of the Black Basses in North America." In *Black Bass Biology and Management*. Washington, DC: Sport Fishing Institute, 1975. Overview of the smallmouth's range.

Mather, Martha E. and Roy A. Stein. "Direct and Indirect Effects of Fish Predation on the Replacement of a Native Crayfish by an Invading Congener." *Canadian Journal of Fisheries and Aquatic Scientists* 50 (1993): 1279–88. Some interesting information on how crayfish aggression deters smallmouth foraging.

McClane, A. J. *The Practical Fly Fisherman*. New York: Prentice-Hall, 1953. Pathbreaking book. Some of the earliest information on modern smallmouth fly fishing.

———. *A. J. McClane's New Standard Fishing Encyclopedia and International Angling Guide*. New York: Holt, Rinehart, and Winston, 1974. Information on smallmouth biology and how-to, with particular attention to fly fishing.

——— and Keith Gardner. *McClane's Game Fish of North America*. New York: Times Books, 1984. Excellent species profile of the smallmouth, with where-to and how-to information.

McNitt, Robert. "Canadarago Lake." *New York Sportsman* (September–October 1985). An Interesting companion piece to Green's study (cf.).

McNeely, David L., Brenda N. Futrell, and Andrew Sih. "An Experimental Study on the Effects of Crayfish on the Predator-Prey Interaction Between Bass and Sculpin." *Oecologia* 85 (1990): 69–73. A fascinating study of the various responses of sculpins to the foraging behavior of smallmouth bass.

Meck, Charles. "White Fly." *Fly Fisherman* (July 1990): 44–47, 68–69. Excellent article on the white fly hatch.

Melner, Samuel and Hermann Kessler, eds. *Great Fishing Tackle Catalogs of the Golden Age*. New York: Crown Publishers, 1972. Insight into the evolution of smallmouth fly patterns from big trout flies to bass bugs.

Miller, Rudolph J. "Comparative Behavior of Centrarchid Basses." In *Black Bass Biology and Management*. Washington, DC: Sport Fishing Institute, 1975.

Morgan, George E. "The Impact of Rock Bass and Sport Fisheries on Smallmouth Bass Communities in Four Central Ontario Oligotrophic Lakes." Haliburton-Hastings Fisheries Assessment Unit, Report No. 92.1. Useful information on the smallmouth's diet.

Murray, Harry. *Fly Fishing for Smallmouth Bass*. New York: Lyons & Burford, 1989. A pathbreaking book.

National Sportsman (June 1922): p. 84. See back cover for different patterns of the Wilder-Dilg minnow.

Nielsen, Larry A. and Donald J. Orth. "The Hellgrammite-Crayfish Bait Fishery of the New River and Its Tributaries, West Virginia." *North American Journal of Fisheries Management* 8: (1988) 317–24. Interesting insights into the "foraging habits" of bait dealers.

Oppel, Frank. *Fishing in North America 1876–1910*. Secaucus, NJ: Castle, 1986. A rich selection of fishing articles from the past.

Outdoor Life. Various issues, 1935–present.

Page, Lawrence M. and Brooks M. Burr. *A Field Guide to Freshwater Fish*, The Peterson Field Guides. Boston: Houghton Mifflin, 1991. An excellent guide for identifying baitfish.

Pennock, Robert. *Freshwater Invertebrates of the United States*. New York: John Wiley and Sons, 1978. See pp. 489–513. Excellent life history of crayfish.

Pfeiffer, C. Boyd. *Bug Making*. New York: Lyons & Burford, 1993. Comprehensive discussion of bugs and poppers, with exceptional illustrations and detailed lists of sources for materials. Includes a complete description of the Messinger method for hair frogs.

Picard, Chris R. and Richard Freitag. "Aspects of Smallmouth Bass, *Micropterus dolomieui*, Life History in Northwestern Ontario, Canada." *Journal of Freshwater Ecology* 8 (1993): 355–60. The relation of population density and growth rate.

Poe, Thomas P., Hal C. Hansel, Steven Vigg, Douglas E. Palmer, and Linda A. Prendergast. "Feeding of Predaceous Fishes on Out-Migrating Juvenile Salmonids in John Day Reservoir, Columbia River." *Transactions of the American Fisheries Society* 120 (1991): 405–20. Interesting information on the limited extent of smallmouth foraging on juvenile salmonids and on the importance of large baitfish.

Probst, W. E., C. F. Rabeni, W. G. Covington, and R. E. Marteney. "Resource Use by Stream-Dwelling Rock Bass and Smallmouth Bass." *Transactions of the American Fisheries Society* 113 (1984): 283–94. Interesting comparative study of the foraging habits of smallmouth and rock bass.

Quinn, Steve. "Angling in the '90s: Tracking Those Wayward Smallmouths." *In-Fisherman* (May–June 1995): 46–60. An exceptional profile of smallmouths in lakes; includes summary and commentary on scientific studies of smallmouth movements in lakes and reservoirs around the country.

Rhead, Louis, ed. *The Basses, Fresh Water and Marine*. New York: F. A. Stokes, 1905.

Ridgway, Mark, Ph.D., fisheries researcher, Algonquin Provincial Park, personal communication, February 1995.

Roell, Michael J. and Donald J. Orth. "Trophic Basis of Production of Stream-Dwelling Smallmouth Bass, Rock Bass, and Flathead Catfish in Relation to Invertebrate Bait Harvest." *Transactions of the American Fisheries Society* 122 (1993): 46–62. Excellent analysis of smallmouth feeding habits.

Scarpino, Philip V. *Great River: An Environmental History of the Upper Mississippi, 1890–1950*. Columbus, OH: University of Missouri Press, 1985. A fascinating discussion of Will Dilg and the beginnings of the Izaak Walton League.

Schiavonne, Al, wildlife biologist, New York State Department of Conservation, pers. comm, January 1994.

Schley, Ben. "Crayfishing River Smallmouths." *Fly Fisherman* (Summer 1982). Excellent discussion of river-fishing tactics. In many ways this was the article that put smallmouths back on the map; the fly ain't bad either.

Schlosser, Isaac J. "Predation Rates and the Behavioral Response of Adult Brassy Minnows (*Hybognathus hankinsoni*) to Creek Chub and Smallmouth Bass Predators." *Copeia* 3 (1988): 691–97. Interesting material on the foraging behavior of stream smallmouths.

Schullery, Paul. *American Fly Fishing: A History*. New York: Lyons & Burford, 1987. Wonderful discussion of the history of smallmouth fly fishing.

Schwiebert, Ernest. *Matching The Hatch*. New York: MacMillan, 1955. Important work on trout.

———. *Nymphs*. New York: Winchester Press, 1973. Excellent information on stoneflies and hellgrammites.

Serns, Steven L. and Michael Hoff. "Food Habits of Adult Yellow Perch and Smallmouth Bass in Nebish Lake, Wisconsin." *Technical Bulletin No. 149*, Wisconsin Department of Natural Resources. Good depiction of seasonal variations in smallmouth diet.

Sports Afield. March 1922.

———. May 1953.

———. Various issues, 1955–75.

Stein, Roy A. and John J. Magnuson. "Behavioral Response of Crayfish to a Fish Predator." *Ecology* 57 (1976): 751–66. Fascinating study of the relationship of smallmouth bass and crayfish.

Stein, Roy A. "Selective Predation, Optimal Foraging, and the Predator-Prey Interaction Between Fish and Crayfish." *Ecology* 58 (1977): 1237–53. An excellent study of selective predation of smallmouths on crayfish.

Stephenson, S. A. and W. T. Momot. "Food Habits and Growth of Walleye, Stizostedion vitreum, Smallmouth Bass, Micropterus dolomieui, and Northern Pike, Esox lucius, in the Kaministiquia River, Ontario." *The Canadian Field-Naturalist* 105 (1991): 517–21. Information on feeding habits.

Sternberg, Richard. *Smallmouth Bass*. Minnetonka, MN: Cy DeCosse, Inc., 1986. Excellent book on all aspects of smallmouth fishing.

Stewart, Richard. *Bass Flies*. Intervale, NH: Northland Press, 1989. Very helpful fly-tying book with first-rate illustrations and instructions.

Stewart, Richard and Farrow Allen. *Flies For Bass & Panfish*. Intervale, NH: Northland Press, 1992. Part of a series of fly-tying books on various species of fish. Exceptional photos and comprehensive list.

Sturgis, William B. *Fly-Tying*. New York: Scribners, 1940. Information on hair bugs, including clipped deer-hair crayfish.

Swisher, Doug and Carl Richards. *Selective Trout*. New York: Lyons & Burford, 1971.

Tapply, H. G. *The Sportsman's Notebook*. New York: Holt, Rinehart, and Winston, 1964. Ahead of its time on fly fishing for smallmouths.

Toth, Michael. *Freshwater Fishing Boats*. New York: Hearst Marine Books, 1995. A fine overview of fishing boats.

Waterman, Charles F. *A History of Angling*. Tulsa, OK: Winchester Press, 1981. Delightful overview of angling history.

————. *Black Bass & the Fly Rod*. Harrisburg, PA: Stackpole, 1993. Technique and history of smallmouth fly rodding.

Index